MISFITS

HOW CREATIVITY IN ADVERTISING SPARKS BRAND GROWTH

ADAM SHERIDAN

Ipsos

www.ipsos.com

First published May 2022

© 2022 Ipsos

ISBN: 978-1-7396844-0-2

PRAISE FOR *MISFITS*

MISFITS provides marketers with an unbiased look at the most important element of their craft – the creative materials that drive customer engagement. So, what constitutes truly ground-breaking advertising? Using real-world examples and scientific rigour, MISFITS skilfully illuminates this question while connecting readers with a framework for rethinking creative impact. The result is an informative and entertaining study that challenges even the most seasoned marketers to re-examine their approach. Adam Sheridan has done a fantastic job of weaving this narrative around a beautifully curated assembly of case studies to entertain savvy marketers and newcomers alike.

Gregory Coleman
Global Head of Marketing
& Franchise at Amazon

In a time in which performance marketing, short-term incentives, attribution models, and the utopian discourse about personalisation have drifted the industry, putting a "stop sign" and re-elevating the importance of creativity to drive effectiveness is paramount. Thanks to Adam and MISFITS for taking the charge onwards, and giving us further tools to continue the recalibration journey.

Ricardo Prieto Ortiz
Specialist Marketing Director, Zone Europe,
Nestle Purina

A compellingly crafted argument for the commercial power of divergent but deeply relevant creativity that prioritises the audience it serves. See MISFITS as your instruction manual for standout ideas that sidestep the status quo.

Paul Kemp-Robertson
Co-founder, Contagious and co-author
of The Contagious Commandments

We now live in a world where advertising platforms have multiplied exponentially and consumers are bombarded with thousands of ads daily. It is critical for brands to develop and execute effective content that will cut through the clutter and engage their target consumers the right way. This book provides a great framework and roadmap to navigate to success.

Ignacio Llaneza
VP Brand & Trade Marketing, Disaronno International LLC

————

Kudos to Adam Sheridan and the entire Ipsos team for the refreshing take on the importance of creativity. True to the title, the author and the book serves as MISFITS in a world where all the focus, attention and money seems to be pushing towards data and Martech. I found that the concept of creativity and its purpose as outlined in MISFITS represented in a very simple and actionable manner. Also, sufficient data has been provided as support for the hypotheses for all us data-hungry practitioners and executives. With several interesting examples and case studies, not limited to advertising (I found the Star Wars case study to be particularly fascinating) and simple tools to inspire and promote creativity, MISFITS can be great reading for students and CMOs alike.

Yuvraj Arora
President, US Categories, Kellogg North America

Creativity is a mindset to empower you to focus on one thing…your audience.

To actively create advertising that surprises, entertains, and is born of empathy for people, reflecting their challenges, their needs, their dreams.

Because the evidence confirms, advertising that delivers this experience is not only more positive for audiences, but also most likely to deliver an increase in sales and market share growth.

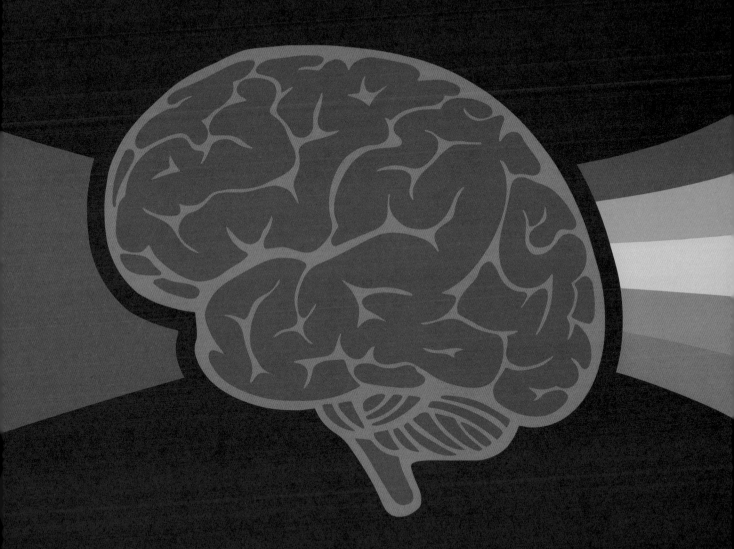

ACKNOWLEDGEMENTS & ABOUT THE AUTHOR

Although I am the named author of this publication, consider me a mere spokesperson for the talented, curious advertising researchers at Ipsos around the globe that have made it possible. It is their expertise and work involving some of the world's most creative advertisers that underpin the evidence and insights we've drawn on.

A special thanks to Dave Walker, Mehrdad Jalali-Ghajar and Ling Ng, who spent countless hours analysing thousands of ads in the Ipsos databank and showed endless patience in entertaining my curiosity and questions. Thanks to Shaun Dix and Arnaud Debia. This publication would not have been possible without your support, encouragement, and passion for creativity.

Thanks also to Colin Strong and Tamara Ansons for the Behavioural Science lens you contributed to the exploratory thinking that led to the myriad of insights we uncovered.

Thanks to our core network of thought leaders and Creative Excellence experts, Eleanor Thornton-Firkin, Pedr Howard, Rachel Rodgers and Keith Glasspoole, for their notes and debate. Thanks also to our activation and design team, Isabelle Fortin, Louise Harrison, Chris Allen and Tessa Balka, who got the publication to its audience and made it look beautiful to behold.

Thanks to the marketers who have given us permission to reference the success of their work to illustrate the trends we have seen: Frank Jeong; Clement Pasquier; Rekha Rao; Scott Campbell; Alberto Greco. Thanks also to our other Ipsos clients and their creative agencies for providing a constant stream of creative work to help us recognise the real value of creativity in advertising.

Thanks to Traci Alford, Juliet Haygarth and Sally Preston at Effie for their partnership and enthusiasm to collaborate on this publication to add to the evidence for the connection between creativity and effectiveness. And of course for their contribution of Effie award winning cases to illustrate the trends and principles we uncovered.

Most importantly, I would also like to thank my wife, Claire, and my daughters, Harriet, and Rosie. Firstly, for supporting me in the crazy idea to journal the things they could hear me talking about on video calls and, secondly, for reminding me of the value of fun and creativity in life.

Adam Sheridan is the Head of Global Products and Analytics for Creative Excellence at Ipsos, where he plays a key role in defining strategy, product portfolio, and thought leadership.

He has two decades of experience in research, specialising in advertising, movies and TV entertainment, measuring the effects of paid advertising to grow brands and content experiences to grow audiences. In addition, he has been a global partner at Ipsos for major digital platforms, helping them understand the user context of their ecosystem and how brands can fully optimise their campaigns to reach end business growth. Adam is a key thought leader at Ipsos and author of several industry recognised papers, identifying the experiences that brands can use to maximise their business outcomes.

These include:

- *The Power of You*. Why distinctive brand assets are a driving force for creative effectiveness.

- *Last Impressions Also Count*. How to evoke an emotional response to leave strong branded memories.

- *We ~~Don't~~ Need to Talk about Ads*. Why only some advertising gets talked about on social media and becomes famous.

- *Selling Creative Research Short?* How creative research can help measure and fuel long term campaign effects.

He has created one advertising campaign in his career, an eBay listing for a second-hand piece of furniture that failed to meet the reserve price.

ABOUT IPSOS

Ipsos is one of the largest market research and polling companies globally, operating in 90 markets and employing over 18,000 people.

Our passionately curious research professionals, analysts and scientists have built unique multi-specialist capabilities that provide true understanding and powerful insights into the actions, opinions and motivations of citizens, consumers, patients, customers or employees. Our 75 business solutions are based on primary data from our surveys, social media monitoring, and qualitative or observational techniques.

Since its creation in 1975, Ipsos revolutionized the media industry with the launch of a tool to measure the effectiveness of billboard advertisements. It was the company's first post-test solution and was soon followed by other post-campaign measurement instruments to target specific media categories.

Today, our experts combine art, science, and knowledge to help our clients achieve their business goals through creative excellence. Building on their know-how, we cover the entire creative development process to help our clients produce award winning and best-in-class advertising.

We also help key brand and marketing decision-makers understand how their brands are performing in their competitive environment to understand the various mechanisms explaining brand growth. We determine and track the most relevant indicators for our clients to inform their brand's strategic plans and define its priority actions.

"Game Changers" – our tagline – summarises our ambition to help our 5,000 clients navigate with confidence our rapidly changing world.

www.ipsos.com

CONTENTS

FOREWORD

Traci Alford,
Global CEO Effie Worldwide

Creating effective marketing is not easy. It requires insight and inspiration. Passion and creativity. Rigour and analysis. All guided by a relentless everyday focus on effectiveness.

At Effie, we celebrate ideas that work, champion progressive thinking, and deliver applicable learnings back into the industry. We find a strong correlation between creativity and driving results in every analysis we have done of our highest performing award winners. There is always a risk of polarisation or downright failure, but our data shows that creatively speaking, fortune favours the bold.

Creating the right conditions for creativity to flourish, developing the right disruptive thinking for your category and quantifying its impact is a challenge for every brand on the planet.

MISFITS helps us to unpack the business of creativity in marketing right now. Not only does it make a compelling case for ideas; it also gives practical insights on how to create them.

It is particularly challenging in the context of the world today. Fast-paced and changeable, we are increasingly reliant on measurement to inform our decisions and give us a sense of certainty. It takes huge confidence for a brand and a boardroom to invest in non-conformist creative ideas.

MISFITS helps us to unpack the business of creativity in marketing right now. Not only does it make a compelling case for ideas; it also gives practical insights on how to create them. It's been a pleasure to work with Adam and the Ipsos team and bring the theory to life with some of the best Effie cases from around the world.

PREFACE

Adam Sheridan

> He was staring at the instruments with the air of one who is trying to convert fahrenheit to centigrade in his head whilst his house is burning down.
>
> **Douglas Adams,** The Hitch Hiker's Guide to the Galaxy

Advertising is an uncertain business, and the business world does not like uncertainty. When CEOs are asked what concerns them about their company's growth prospects, economic uncertainty is in the top three things that keep them awake at night[1].

And amidst such uncertainty, their attitude to advertising is clear in their actions. When the weather is fair, advertising is a brand investment and an important tool for growth. However, when economic clouds appear, it morphs into an expendable cost, removed to protect the bottom line and help regain a sense of control, until the horizon clears, pointing to better days ahead[2].

Yet the evidence suggests this mindset can hamper market share growth, as businesses that cut advertising spending in times of recession achieve less growth in subsequent years than those that maintain or increase it[3]. Procter & Gamble, who are well known for evidence based decision-making in brand management, often "double down" on advertising investments during such uncertain periods, though examples of such companies are few and far between[4].

Despite clear evidence for its ability to generate growth, why then is advertising treated by most companies in such a volatile and expendable way? The answer lies not in the world of business, but

DON'T
PANIC

in human nature. That businesses are managed by people, and people tend to gravitate towards the familiar. To manage risk and focus on immediate value to achieve more certain outcomes, despite paving the way for competitors to gain more market share in subsequent years.

More specifically in advertising, this human need to see more certain, short-term results within often forensically examined budgets is embodied by a growing focus on managing media budgets more efficiently. Advances in computing power and data storage have facilitated a greater range of capabilities in media targeting and personalisation, and access to more volumes of data, more immediately. This

constant stream of data helps marketers measure views, interactions, and conversions they have achieved, and in turn, meet the very human need to increase a feeling of certainty and tangible outcomes.

While efficiently managing a media budget is undoubtedly important, this can distract from the real objective of advertising: to increase sales and market share gains. If the quality of the experience being delivered to the audience is not effective enough to influence behaviour, does it really matter how efficiently they are reached in the first place?

This growing attention on a hoard of media data at the expense of creating an effective advertising

experience is akin to a spaceship travelling across the Universe quickly while pondering the reason for it. It is unlikely when writing *The Hitch Hiker's Guide to the Galaxy* that Douglas Adams would have intended a comparison to marketing efficiency and effectiveness, though themes in the book do represent the universal tension in human nature that advertising needs to overcome.

In the book, the protagonist Arthur is saved by his alien friend Ford Prefect from the destruction of Earth, thus triggering a journey across the Universe and discovery of its true purpose and meaning. At one point, Arthur and Ford are hurtling across the universe in a spaceship piloted by Slartibartfast. The

pilot has an array of instruments to chart their course and stares at the screen, near mesmerised by all the readings, only to realise that he needs to re-focus his mind on the reason for their journey, which is to save the Universe. In this respect, we can draw parallels to the predicament faced in advertising today. That because of the human need to be certain of any outcome, irrespective of its value, we are focusing on measures of Fahrenheit and Centigrade while the house of the advertising experience is burning.

And the response of many creative agencies to keep the house intact has been to promote the value of "creativity". To highlight the value of ideas, stories and the craft of advertising to fuel end business effects. But the problem with this position is that creativity as a concept is wrapped in ambiguity and uncertainty, without a relatable frame of reference that businesspeople under shareholder scrutiny can understand.

This publication aims to help move beyond the impasse by proposing a paradox. That embracing the uncertainty of creativity when producing advertising is the most certain way to achieve strong business returns in the short and long term.

We make the case for this paradox by outlining a definition and shared language of what creativity means in advertising, not only from an industry perspective but also from the standpoint of regular people, the audience that advertising needs to influence. With this language in hand, we draw on evidence identifying the relationship between the core elements of creativity and advertising effects. We then frame this evidence in the achievements of the Misfits of the world, the modern-day creators, the innovators and the people that embrace uncertainty by *not fitting in* and use this mindset to their advantage, contrary to the assumption the more familiar and certain approach is the most effective.

In outlining this evidence and shared language of creativity, we aim to arm creative agencies and marketers with the facts they need to give people that make campaign investment decisions more security. That the evidence confirms embracing uncertainty and trusting in a Misfit mindset to pursue extraordinary work is a surer way to realise stronger business effects than buying work that feels familiar and safe.

What we do not attempt is to provide a magic formula for advertising success. Promising this would be fanciful and implausible because, as we will see, what represents creativity and fuels advertising effects is not one specific magic ingredient, but a mindset and openness to apply and combine different things that, if used well, can often deliver business success.

By making the case for a Misfit mindset, we also hope the people involved in the creation of advertising can harness the value of creativity in their work more regularly and intensely. Because this is the foundation of the advertising house to deliver sales and market share growth for brands.

.

WE NEED TO TALK ABOUT CREATIVITY

The role of the Chief Marketing Officer has become increasingly ambiguous and insecure. When asked how well defined they think their role is, only 37% agree it is "very clear"[5]. And the average tenure of a CMO has decreased from four years to just over three since 2014[6]. This opaqueness of responsibilities and reduced lifespan of the CMO role is unsurprising and attributed in large part to the opportunity and complexity brought with the new world order of data enabled media placement.

Long gone are the days when the role of a marketer was solely about the management of brands, to think carefully and dutifully about the role the brand plays in the lives of people, and how best to get that brand in the hands and homes of those it can help. Although this does remain a staple part of the role, responsibilities and attention have since extended to the opportunity of data managed media and customer relationships.

Marketers have never before had access to more data on their customers and prospective customers to plan and track immediate interactions and behavioural responses to their campaigns.

According to the investment trends, this is where the attention is moving to, with data from Gartner highlighting that budgets in Martech infrastructure are rising (22% to 26%) while spending with external agency services have moved in the opposite direction (25% to 22%)[7]. On the surface, these movements in advertising investment make sense, from a business and a human perspective.

The business case for assigning more resources to the data world is compelling. By applying the context of data and leveraging a range of media channels to reach and target the right people, marketers can more efficiently act and measure the outcomes of their investments, often in near real time. This combination of speed and efficiency is particularly attractive because it can enable marketers in less stable roles to demonstrate a return on advertising investments more quickly and more frequently.

Let us also represent a revolutionary idea from a human perspective. Marketers are people. Yes, people. People with mortgages. People with children to support. People with the desire to do what their culture has taught them since they were children, to achieve success and gain approval.

With that bomb dropped, let us expand on why, as people, marketers are wired to turn their attention to these immediate data streams and the media placement of advertising at the expense of the creation of advertising itself.

FIGURE 1: MARKETING BUDGET ALLOCATIONS ACROSS RESOURCE ALLOCATIONS

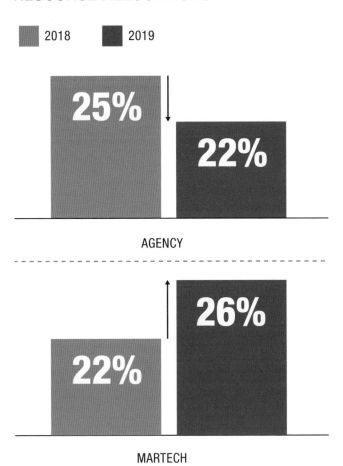

2018   2019

25%   22%

AGENCY

22%   26%

MARTECH

n = 326 North America/U.K respondents (2019); n = 605 (2018); Source: Gartner CMO Spend Survey Q: How is your company's fiscal year 2019 total marketing expense budget being allocated to or spend on major resource categories?

The creation of advertising is an inherently uncertain business. You can work with an agency to identify a core idea, develop executions and use research services to market test the resulting work. But once you embark on the process from a creative brief to launching your campaign, you are not certain about what will happen.

You don't know if people will even take the time to view your campaign, let alone encode it in their minds and help you to later influence moments of choice.

And as human beings, we don't like uncertainty. In fact, our brains have evolved to reduce uncertainty. As the renowned neuroscientist and founder of the "Lab of Misfits" Beau Lotto says, *"Almost any living system evolves to deal with uncertainty and the ambiguity of data. If early humans weren't sure that a predator was a predator it was usually too late. They became dinner"*[8]. In practical terms today, this means that as people, our brains interpret the information and stimulus around us to construct perception, to create certainty from uncertain experiences.

There is a range of perception experiments providing evidence that our brains don't simply receive information from the world but interpret it. One example in Figure 2 is a stimulus used in experiments by Stanley Coren[9]. What do you see?

Based on the results of Coren's experiments, it is likely you will have seen a triangle. But you did not see it, you interpreted it, automatically with little cognitive effort. However, all that is on the page or screen are pixels and shapes that your brain is connecting and identifying based on your past experiences. Why did you not instead see three images of Pacman, all descending on the centre, looking for the next Ghost to vanquish? Maybe you did, but this would be because, like the author, you have played a lot of Pacman, and your past experiences influenced your perception.

FIGURE 2:

Source: Stanley Coren[9]

While perception and subsequent behaviour are often influenced by past experiences, processed in our minds automatically, we are not completely governed by the past. If this were the case, we would never have left the areas surrounding our caves when searching for food or developed the complex social and societal structures of government and commerce that underpin our lives today.

Instead, as people, we can also deliberately assess less familiar options and information. Ipsos ran research experiments in partnership with the Child Development and Educational Psychology Laboratory, LaPsyDe, and Temple University[10] suggesting that we switch between automatic and deliberate modes of processing on a mindful to mindless continuum[11].

While the continuum model suggests we can switch to more deliberate processing, this often depends on an intervention or external influence, such as socio-cultural context. As people, we may want to move to more green and sustainable behaviours, such as buying an electric car, but this will often depend on an intervention, such as government grant schemes to change our ingrained behaviour of using fossil fuel cars.

FIGURE 3: MINDFUL TO MINDLESS CONTINUUM

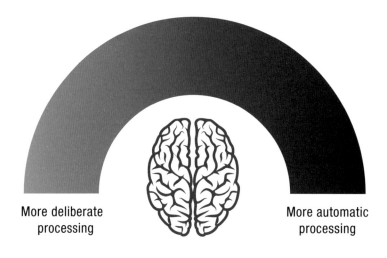

More deliberate processing

More automatic processing

Source: Ipsos[11]

With a dependency on intervention, this means that people will mostly gravitate to familiar options and repeat past behaviours, making "safe" decisions, even if this is at the expense of pursuing the most effective option. In fact, we have built structures and systems to actively favour the familiar, to promote and cultivate conformity in our lives.

From birth, our lives are mapped out in a pre-determined sequence of events, designed to eliminate uncertainty from the equation of thought and decision-making. From the age of four, we are placed in a school system which is designed to make children focus on the next step, the next grade. A system that encourages a focus on a uniform, standardised outcome in the next test or scorecard. And if we want schools to be places where young people can express themselves and explore new ideas and ways of thinking to get to more effective outcomes, the evidence of the cultural environment in the school system is not reassuring. When teachers are asked if they enjoy having creative children in their classroom, most agree with this statement, but when asked about their opinion of individual students, they are more likely to disapprove or dislike those who scored highly on creativity tests[12].

What this environment and culture we place our children in from an early age means is that we learn to conform, we learn to fit in. Because we can succeed by fitting in and gaining the approval of others. And this quest for approval to progress in the journey of life does not end when we leave the school system. It pervades the corporate environment, with studies identifying that while company decision-makers agree creativity is an important goal, they are more likely to reject creative ideas they had not seen before[13].

Other academic studies that expand on why people reject creativity, despite claiming they are favourable towards it, point to the influence of the human need to manage uncertainty. In an experiment designed to isolate uncertainty when deciding on a creative or more familiar idea, people were placed in an uncertain condition, where they were unaware of the incentive they might receive, were more likely to express a bias towards familiar over creative ideas than those who knew the incentive they would receive[14]. In effect, they gravitated to the familiar to manage the uncertainty they faced, although the uncertainty of the incentive was not linked to the ideas they judged.

These observations about human nature and our inherent need to extinguish uncertainty from our lives bring us back to the shifts we see in advertising investment and what this means for the industry.

In the world of commerce, there are perhaps few things more uncertain than the return you will make on an at times multi-million dollar advertising campaign, and if we're wired to remove uncertainty from the equation of our decision-making with conformity and approval, it stands to reason that marketers would run to the realms of immediate, abundant media data to turn in their score cards to their management.

But this Martech nirvana the industry is moving towards is not bereft of consequences. Firstly, the focus on immediate interactions and cost management of media buys provides value in terms of efficiency, not effectiveness. A focus that Will Lion, Joint Chief Strategy Officer at BBH, coined the *"efficiency bubble"*, a dynamic where more resources and attention are assigned to reach more people, more frequently, more efficiently, conflating this with the real goal to increase effectiveness, by growing market share and selling more products[15].

Access to data management systems and digital media data is also democratic. If every company that advertises has access to every system and invests their resources to master it in the quest for greater efficiency, they will all reach the same place, a media singularity where no one company holds an advantage over another in their advertising investments.

And what a delicious irony, with marketers chasing new media channels they are not sure will work, yet seemingly moving away from investing in the production of original and different content that is placed there.

It does make sense,because the efficiency they target as an objective can often be measured in impressions and views quickly. Yet investing in creativity to produce the content itself to drive effectiveness is less certain and instantly measurable, with sales lift and brand tracking data often carrying a lag of weeks or months after the campaign has launched.

Which brings us back to advertising and creativity. If companies that invest in the production and placement of advertising are moving more towards data and media management at the expense of the resources they put into making it, what is the evidence to suggest that they must reconsider and rebalance their budgets? That creative ideas and experiences are the only real competitive advantage marketers can invest in to grow their brands and win market share? Moreover, does the quality of the advertising experience even matter? And what role, if any, does creativity play in the delivery of that experience?

There is evidence available to us that suggests creative quality does indeed matter. That if you send something bereft of strategy or production quality

FIGURE 4: SHAREMARKET PERFORMANCE

AVERAGE ANNUAL SHARE
PRICE GROWTH 1999-2015

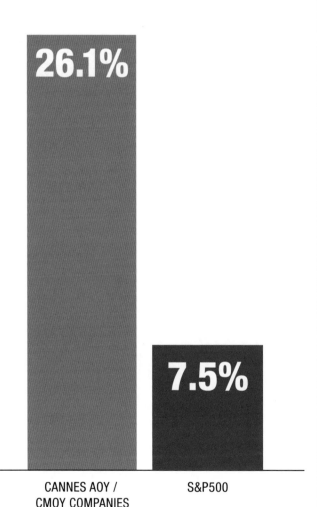

26.1%

7.5%

CANNES AOY /   S&P500
CMOY COMPANIES

Source: James Hurman[16]

down the media pipes, it does not matter how quickly or in how many ways you send it. It will just not be as effective as it could have otherwise been.

James Hurman's celebrated work *The Case for Creativity* includes an analysis highlighting the value of creativity in a language business decision-makers understand: the stock market. In his analysis, Hurman makes a link between companies that are awarded the Cannes' Creative Marketer of the Year award with their stock market performance. Being awarded by a jury of peers as the most creative marketer of the year means that you are consistently pursuing creative work, particularly moreover a creative culture. If there is business value by focusing more energy and resources on creative advertising, we would expect to observe a link with subsequent stock market performance, which Hurman duly does. With those companies given the award x3.5 more likely to outperform the S&P500 growth average[16].

This analysis also points to the need to consider the business impact of advertising more in the long term, with the period of time in Hurman's analysis accounting for six years of subsequent growth. A quite different concept of time compared to the short-term campaign by campaign or even day-by-day scorecards more companies are today demanding from their marketers and investing in the Martech infrastructure to facilitate.

While there is evidence that advertising considered to be "creative" is linked to real business value, let us, for now, put ourselves in the shoes of a financial officer or CEO, whose responsibility is end cost management and growth. If they are presented with this evidence, how compelling is it really in the corporate boardroom, where certainty is so prized?

On the one hand, the link to the stock market is relatable and motivating for financial decision-makers. If they invest in the agency talent and time to produce good quality advertising, they will profit from this in their company value. There is little not to like. But this type of evidence can be questioned.

The most obvious is that it is a correlation, not causality. Are the winners of the most creative marketer award performing well in the stock market because they are investing in creative advertising, or are their successes in other areas of their business simply allowing for more budget to be made available to increase their share of voice in the category, even if their advertising is mediocre?

Another question is the validity of creative awards themselves as a measure of advertising quality. While we strongly believe in the value of creative awards for the industry at large and the promotion of good quality advertising and experiences, we need to consider this question: can an analysis of award entrants and winners fully reflect the value of creativity to advertising more generally? One would think that if an agency or brand has gone to the trouble of entering a creative awards process, they have already invested in the process of developing their advertising with creativity in mind. If all cases have had a deliberate investment in creativity and a goal to produce good quality advertising, can comparing entrants and winners be a reliable indication of the value of creativity in advertising overall?

We also need to consider if when judging award entrants, juries of advertising professionals can objectively assess a campaign on its qualities often a year after it has launched, in some cases to industry fanfare and acclaim. This is not a criticism in any form of awards juries. They consist of some of the brightest

talents the industry has to offer, but like marketers, jury members are people, and people, as we have seen, are conditioned and prone to conformity. Even if, ironically, this means they are conforming to a preceding narrative that a campaign is strongly creative.

This brings us to the definition of creativity itself. The eagle-eyed readers amongst you will have noticed that we are yet to offer a clear definition of creativity. We have made implicit links to it representing something different or unfamiliar, though we have not been more specific. This is deliberate and represents the challenge agencies have to demonstrate the business value of creativity and awards juries have in judging if it is there or not. If there is no shared definition and language as to what creativity is, how can awards be relied upon as a measure of advertising quality?

What these questions point to is a need for more evidence to help business decision-makers understand what creativity is, and when they know what it is, what contribution it plays to the quality of the advertising itself. To build on the signals of the value of creativity from awards database analysis to advertising more generally. By understanding the role of creativity in a more representative sample of advertising, we can help agencies and marketers build a stronger case for the investment in time and resources to make advertising, rather than only the pipes used to deliver and monitor it.

And we need to draw this evidence from the perceptions and advertising effects observed among regular people. The people that advertising is tasked to influence and change the behaviour of to increase brand sales and market share. The people that, like marketers, care about their mortgages and supporting their children, but unlike marketers, don't care a lot about advertising and brands.

> **What these questions point to is a need for more evidence to help business decision-makers understand what creativity is, and when they know what it is, what contribution it plays to the quality of the advertising itself.**

SUMMARY

- Marketers are under increasing pressure to demonstrate the business value of their activities. They are investing more in Martech infrastructure to place media and gain access to more data, more quickly to demonstrate value, while investing less in creating the advertising they place.

- Marketers are people. People have evolved to manage uncertainty in their lives by automatically and efficiently repeating past choices and behaviours. To manage uncertainty and make safe decisions, people have been conditioned by systems and structures to favour the familiar and conform to existing expectations.

- The investment of creating and placing advertising is an uncertain business. Data driven media placement and short-term spend monitoring provide more certainty than a belief in the long term value of creative ideas and executions.

- While a greater focus on media placement and monitoring can enable efficiency gains, it is not guaranteed to fuel effectiveness.

- Data and access to digital media platforms is democratic. Everyone can access and master them, meaning everyone is heading to the same media singularity in the quest for efficiency.

- The case for creativity has been made by connecting creative award winners to their financial performance. But this can be questioned by people in the corporate boardroom as it does not represent advertising more generally.

- There is no singular definition of creativity. If there is no shared definition and language, there is no meaningful discussion to be had about how to use it and the business value it delivers.

- We need to define what creativity means and how it contributes to advertising effects more generally to make the case to invest more time and resources in it. We need to do this by examining evidence based on the responses of regular people, rather than only industry opinion.

CREATIVITY: MOVING BEYOND THE RORSCHACH OF ADVERTISING

Despite being a widely pursued endeavour, there is little agreement as to what "creativity" is and why it matters. In technology, the focus tends to be on "innovation", the application of different capabilities to improve or underpin new solutions. For psychologists, it is a cognitive process and aptitude that can be amplified or constrained by environmental conditions. In the arts, it is the creation of a new, never before seen experience.

This range of meanings and applications of the word is the result of its evolution and use over time in language and culture. The first use of the word "creativity" is thought to have been in Christian religious texts, specifically *The Book of Genesis*, where the focus was on the world's creation by God[17]. In this sense, we as people were not considered capable of creating anything, more discovering what God had already created and interpreting that in works such as paintings and sculpture.

The deference of creativity to God started to change from the 15th century onwards in the age of the Renaissance, where there was a growing focus on the work and accomplishments of individuals during this period. A recognition that people could create things of value and that humanity, in general, could gain and apply knowledge for its own advancement. Although creativity leapt from the divine to mortals in this time, it was often associated with "special" or talented people,

geniuses who would create scientific or artistic work that would reshape the perceptions and lives of society.

And there is perhaps no better example of the connection between creativity and genius than Leonardo Da Vinci. The archetypal polymath applied new ways of thinking across science and art that opened the minds of people to the possibility of human flight, while also captivating the imagination to this very day with the androgynous and ambiguous Mona Lisa.

While the interweaving of genius and creativity pervades in the modern day, with Albert Einstein and Pablo Picasso being popular examples, it's only in the 19th century that creativity also takes on a more inclusive, yet mechanistic meaning, with the emergence of the social science of psychology. In this study of creativity, the concept is considered a process, a way of thinking that has the possibility to identify and develop new solutions of value.

A popular theoretical model of creativity that moves towards a recognition that anyone can apply such thinking is "Big C and small c"[18]. In this model, the Big C relates to more transformational and eminent creativity that can change the world. An example of such eminent creativity is Edison's light bulb or Einstein's general theory of relativity. On a smaller and more accessible scale is the small c, a way of

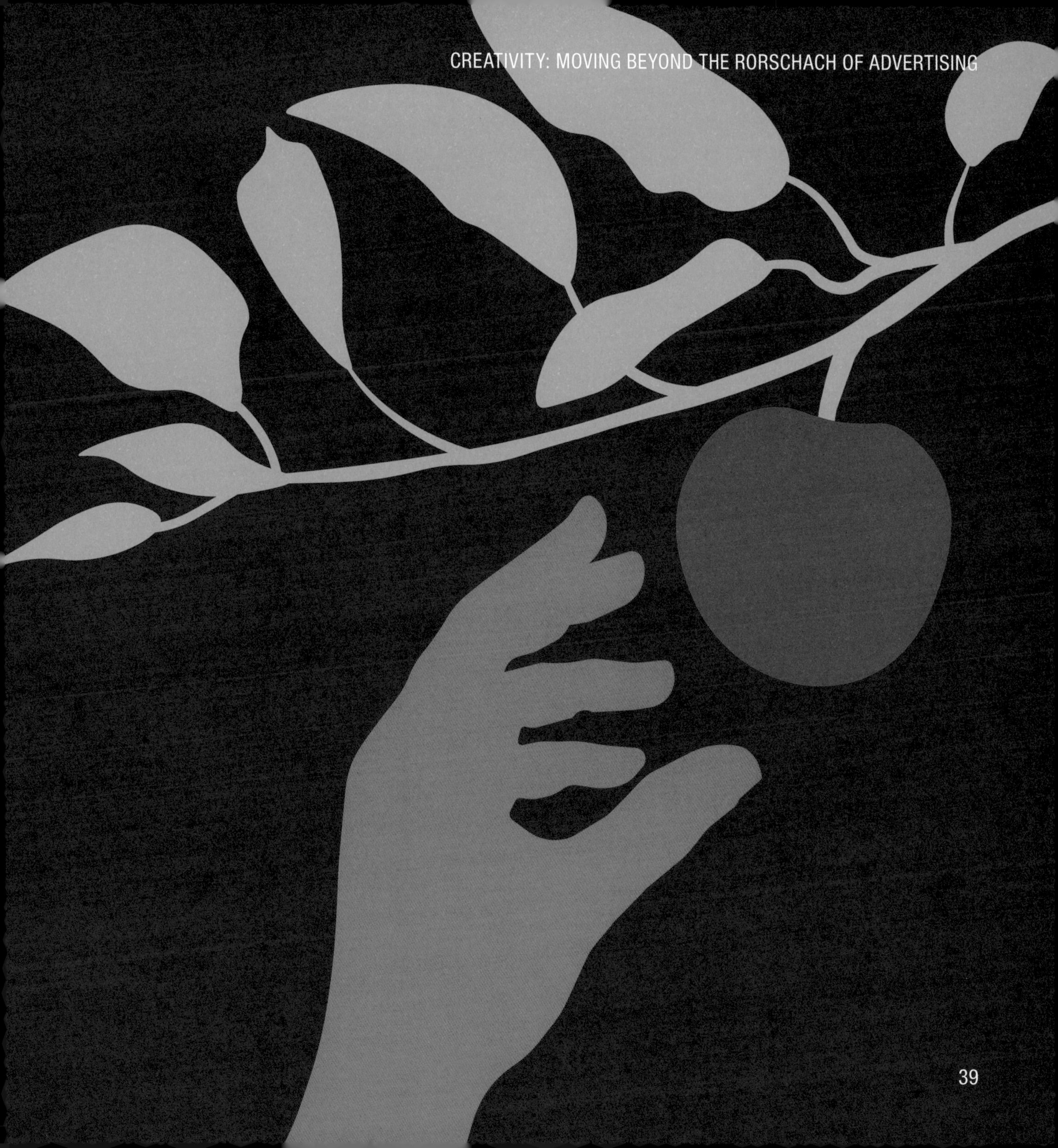

thinking that anyone can learn and apply to their everyday lives, thus facilitating the optimisation of outcomes. In the modern day, this more inclusive small c definition of creativity is now generally accepted and pursued as a way of thinking or collaborating in a range of environments, from educational to corporate.

When charting these different uses and interpretations of creativity in the modern day, it's clear that the word "creativity" is somewhat of a Rorschach in language amid the pursuit of human improvement. What these interpretations do though appear to have in common is the concept of originality or novelty, whether this is in applying something familiar in a new way or creating something new that has not been seen before. Another key dimension is the usefulness or quality of the novelty, meaning it must have some form of utility or relevancy to the end user. In this sense, an original idea, artistic expression or technical capability is not considered to be "creative" unless it has some form of usefulness, fulfilling the emotional or functional needs of the target audience. A new expression in art is not particularly creative if few people want to see it, just like a new technical development lacks creativity if nobody wants to use it.

One industry where the failure of originality without utility seems to be on a repeat cycle is electric mobility. When launched in 1985, the Sinclair C5 could certainly be considered "original". There was no other mobility device like it, able to transport one person, by means of electric power. The problem was that it was a rather cumbersome, slow means of transport and it made anyone using it look rather ridiculous. Future generations of personal mobility repeated the same trap of newness over usefulness, such as the original Segway, where the rider had to lean in the direction of travel. Another "original" way of travel that was difficult to use and made the person using it look rather silly, so much so that its most familiar reference today is as the trusty steed of Paul Blart in the comedy movie *Mall Cop*. The modern-day incarnation of e-scooters appears to be moving towards a more useful application, with more compact frames for use on roads, though even these devices attract a polarised response from people and legislatures alike while continuing to make some people look a bit silly when using them.

If we accept the concept of creativity depends on a combination of originality and usefulness or some form of end value to the audience based on these successes and failures in applying creative thinking, what does this mean in the context of modern-day advertising? If we move beyond the humble musings of an advertising researcher to the people who pursue the path of creativity and make advertising, how do they define creativity? Having summarised some psychological models of creativity and creative thinking, let us now turn to the creativity models promoted by advertisers and their agencies.

Heineken is one of the biggest advertiser spenders worldwide, with over 250 brands and a global staff of more than 1,500 marketers. Alongside this investment and commitment to advertising is a recognition that creativity is a key asset to their success in developing advertising that delivers business effects, with their former Senior Director of Global Marketing Capability, Cinzia Morelli-Verhoog, describing it as *"part of the company DNA...to drive engagement with consumers"*[19]. Their creative ladder is a key instrument Heineken use in their effort to ensure creativity is in the DNA of their advertising.

The role of the ladder is to have a universal reference point for what creativity is, and what their advertising needs to aim for as an end outcome. The ladder has a scale from 1-10, with 1 labelled as "Destructive" and 10 as "Legendary". In this ladder, we see some clues as to what Heineken consider to be the essence of creativity, with attributes such as "Fresh" ranked higher than "Cliché" and "Ground-breaking" and "Contagious" ranked further up the ladder. Across these words, we see a recognition that originality and novelty are key, as well as some form of value such as being

FIGURE 5: THE HEINEKEN CREATIVE LADDER

10	LEGENDARY
9	CULTURAL PHENOMENOM
8	CONTAGIOUS
7	GROUNDBREAKING
6	FRESH
5	OWNABLE
4	CLICHÉ
3	CONFUSING
2	HIJACKED
1	DESTRUCTIVE

Source: Fast Company[19]

discussion-worthy, with a focus on popularity and social currency. Another well-known creative ladder is the Leo Burnett HumanKind Scale that also takes a 1-10 scale approach as a reference point for what their agency should aim for in the work they deliver to brands. Like the Heineken creative ladder, it starts with "Destructive" as the lowest point of the scale, though the word "Change" is used frequently, from "Changes the way people think and feel" to "Changes the world" instead of using words like Legendary and Contagious

at the upper end of the scale. With this use of the word "Change", we see a recognition of the role of advertising to change perception or behaviour that is to the advantage of the brand, implicitly suggesting there needs to be some form of value for the advertiser and the audience in the experience delivered.

Examples of creative ladders of this type then appear to be an effective tool for marketers in large organisations to have a common language around

FIGURE 6: THE LEO BURNETT HUMANKIND SCALE

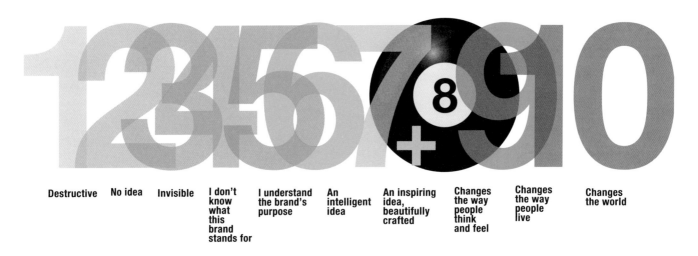

Source: Leo Burnett

what creativity means to them, and to promote a culture of creativity in their organisation. They are also likely underpinned by more detailed tools and playbooks to implement the principles into tangible marketing campaigns. However, they do come with a central dependency, that the organisation using them already believes in the power of creativity and agree on the elements driving it. Companies like Heineken clearly have this belief and commitment, though some advertisers have yet to take this step, perhaps in part because they are unsure as to what creativity is and how it can help drive their business outcomes.

At this point, let us turn to how the thought leaders in the creative agency world define creativity. The people who plan and produce advertising for a living. While it's somewhat ludicrous to claim we can represent all the diverse opinions of creativity across the advertising industry, two themes are apparent: one focused mainly on originality and difference; another that considers interaction between originality and relevancy, or value, to the target audience.

In the originality and difference camp, Dan Wieden of Wieden+Kennedy takes a near rebellious approach to the definition and application of creativity, using words such as "chaos"[20]:

Chaos is the only thing that honestly wants you to grow. The only friend who really helps you be creative.

In a similar vein, the photographer of the famed and controversial Benetton campaigns, Oliviero Toscani, uses words such as "disturbing" and "subversive"[21]:

Creativity is Genesis: birth, divine force, energy, imagination, suffering, commitment, faith, generosity. Creativity has to be visionary, subversive, disturbing. It must be innovative. It must drive ideas and concepts.

The renowned Bill Bernbach, the co-founder of DDB, also took a similar view that advertising that is memorable needs to "break" things[22]:

Rules are what the artist breaks; the memorable never emerged from a formula.

Across these opinions in the originality and difference camp, we see a theme focused on the value of difference, of breaking things and standing out. What then of the camp that considers a need for interaction between difference and relevancy?

By contrast, Sir John Hegarty takes a more nuanced view when describing the role of creativity in advertising in his book, *Hegarty on Advertising: Turning Intelligence Into Magic*, stating that *"If you question something you need to answer it, with sincerity"*[23]. Here, we see an appreciation of the need to move beyond difference and originality alone, and to also offer an alternative discourse or message, one the advertiser believes in with "sincerity".

Having observed a recognition of the need to enact "Change" in the Leo Burnett HumanKind Scale, it is unsurprising to also note that Burnett himself makes the case for relevancy or end value to the audience when considering creativity:

"Creativity is the art of establishing new and meaningful relationships between previously unrelated things in a manner that is relevant, believable and in good taste, but which somehow presents the product in a fresh new light"[24].

With the words "in good taste", Burnett also alludes to the value of a good quality experience for the audience. While this interacts with difference, originality and some form of relevancy, it is interesting to see a recognition that part of creative advertising is simply offering an experience that is appreciated or enjoyed.

In his book *Why Does the Pedlar Sing?* Paul Feldwick elaborates on this theme, making the case for creativity and effectiveness in advertising being present when it is *"not just a pitch, but a performance"*. And while Feldwick openly states that *"a great performance doesn't automatically maximize revenues or profits"*[25], he provides a compelling case history of famous campaigns that have placed an importance on entertaining audiences, while also delivering success in terms of in-market campaign effects. In this context, he cites the example of Barclaycard campaign series with Rowan Atkinson. A campaign that was not necessarily the result of careful planning and strategy, or an attempt to be different for the sake of difference, but more happenstance in leveraging a new character Atkinson was developing, an idiotic government spy

who delivered slapstick laughter by obstinately never considering the use of the features of Barclaycard, thereby leading to his downfall. Incidentally, this character was also the genesis of Atkinson's movie character Johnny English, further pointing to the shared experience between effective advertising and entertainment content that Feldwick proposes.

Across these thought leaders, we then see two interpretations of what creativity means in advertising. One focuses on difference in a rebellious or renegade fashion, whereas the other considers difference or originality blended with something of relevancy or value to the target audience, be that the messages delivered, entertainment, talkability or a combination of all the above.

FIGURE 7: DIVIDE IN THE AD INDUSTRY ON WHAT CREATIVITY MEANS IN ADVERTISING

Chaos is the only thing that honestly wants you to grow. The only friend who really helps you be creative.[I]

Dan Wieden

Rules are what the artist breaks; the memorable never emerged from a formula.[II]

Bill Bernbach

The art of establishing new and meaningful relationships between previously unrelated things in a manner that is relevant, believable and in good taste, but which somehow presents the product in a fresh new light.[IV]

Leo Burnett

*At heart, creativity is about breaking rules, not sticking to them…
The skill for us in marketing communication is balance. We need to manage this tension between difference and similarity, pattern and distinctiveness.[V]*

Les Binet

Creativity is Genesis: birth, divine force, energy, imagination, suffering, commitment, faith, generosity. Creativity has to be visionary, subversive, disturbing. It must be innovative. It must drive ideas and concepts.[III]

Oliviero Toscani

I. http://wklondon.com/2005/02/words_from_wied/

II. https://medium.com/@Aaricia.wiesen/context-reseach-5c12de1d759c

III. Oliviero Toscani: More Than Fifty Years of Magnificent Failures, Oliviero Toscani (2015)

IV. https://medium.com/leos-words-of-wisdom/what-is-creativity-605547083dcd

V. How not to plan – 66 ways to screw it up, Les Binet and Sarah Carter (2018)

VI. Ogilvy on Advertising, David Ogilvy (2011)

VII. Hegarty on Advertising: Turning Intelligence into Magic, John Hegarty (2011)

It's not creative unless it sells.[VI]

David Ogilvy

If you question something you need to answer it, with sincerity.[VII]

John Hegarty

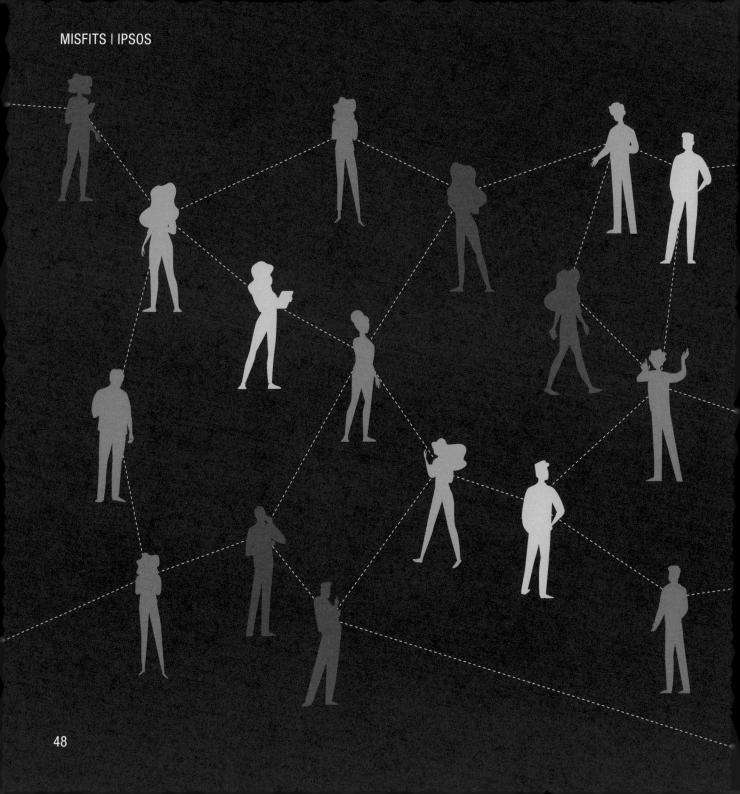

We will not judge which is right or wrong, though let us return to the perceptions of the people who approve advertising investments. As we have identified, marketers and key financial decision-makers are people at the end of the day. People are wired and culturally conditioned to reduce or fully remove uncertainty from their lives. In this context, which interpretation of creativity might be more effective in persuading decision-makers to invest in truly creative work? The one of originality and rebellion or the one where originality is blended with relevancy, sincerity and an appreciated or enjoyed performance?

Even if one interpretation is more accepted than another, we need to ask which is the more effective version of creativity that marketers should pursue to reach the strongest business effects from their advertising investments. Chaos and originality alone may be more uncomfortable to pursue, but if you take this approach, is it perhaps more effective than pursuing relevancy and sincerity alongside newness?

At this point, we will turn to the perceptions of people. Not the people who create advertising, but regular everyday people. The people who think very little about advertising but whose behaviours can often be influenced by its experience.

Ipsos ran a survey of over 20,000 people, representing eight countries, and asked them to describe creative advertising they have seen before, using the below question:

Some advertising is described as "creative". What words or phrases come to mind when you think about creative advertising you have seen?"

The answers provided were diverse and illuminating. A theme of difference and originality did indeed strongly come through, with words like "unique" and "different" most frequently used, though other themes also emerged, such as "fun", "entertaining" and offering "joy" and "happiness" as well as "good quality." This, in turn, echoed Feldwick's case for the value of a good performance that entertains, and Burnett's for one that is appreciated and of good taste.

We also see a strong theme of "informative/ interesting". The responses underpinning this theme were not more specific among enough people to break it out further, though what we can consider from this is that people connect creativity in advertising to useful information that helps or educates them in some way, likely alongside a different, original, and entertaining experience.

FIGURE 8: HOW REGULAR PEOPLE DESCRIBE CREATIVE ADVERTISING THEY HAVE SEEN

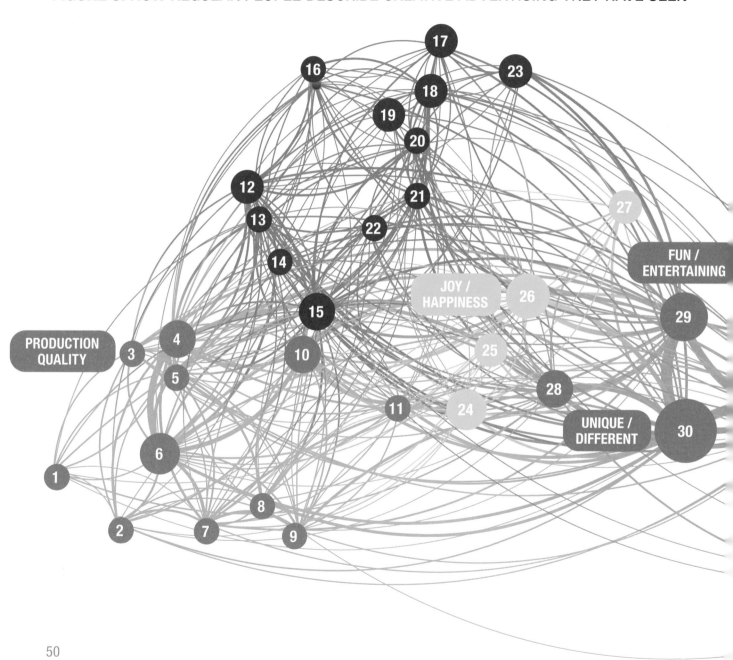

1 cartoon

2 animation

3 character

4 music

5 image

6 colour

7 use

8 quality

9 technology

10 lot

11 imagination

12 commercial

13 phrase

14 word

15 life

16 long time

17 moment

18 creative ad

19 nothing

20 example

21 song

22 consumer

23 surprise

24 advert

25 feeling

26 joy/happiness

27 everyone

28 good/quality

29 fun/entertaining

30 unique/different

31 interesting/
informative

32 box/
out-of-the-box

31 **INTERESTING /
INFORMATIVE**

32

*Source: Ipsos poll of n=20,578 across: Argentina;
Brazil; Canada; China; Mexico; South Africa; UK; USA.*

In these responses, we see alignment with the more nuanced camp in advertising, the thought leaders who are of the view that originality needs to be accompanied by value, whether this is an entertaining experience, one that is relevant and useful in some form, or a combination of these elements. Again, this does not imply that the more rebellious proposition is without merit, that chaos or disturbance is not of inherent value to the creative process. Only that regular people consider the end experience of advertising is creative if it is both original and valuable to them in some form, whether this is entertainment or something useful to them.

And while we should not consider the perceptions of regular people as the singular "truth" of what creativity is in advertising, we do consider that the definition should at least in part reflect the audience it needs to influence. Accordingly, in the remainder of this publication, we will reference our proposed definition of creativity in advertising, "an original or different experience that is valued by the end audience".

Our goal in proposing this definition is not to claim a vernacular on the definition of creativity in general. As we have observed, the advertising industry is replete with many definitions and opinions and one cannot be considered "right" and another "wrong". Instead, with this definition, we aim to represent the experience of people and the target audiences of advertising, to understand if this blend of originality and value is related in any way to end short-term sales effects and long term market share growth.

Before exploring these relationships in the context of advertising effects, let us first reflect on the Misfits of the world. The people who embrace uncertainty and do not fit. If as people, we are all naturally wired to conform and make decisions based on our past assumptions, what happens when we break free of convention, and what can we learn from this in terms of the creation of advertising and achieving the end business effects it exists to deliver?

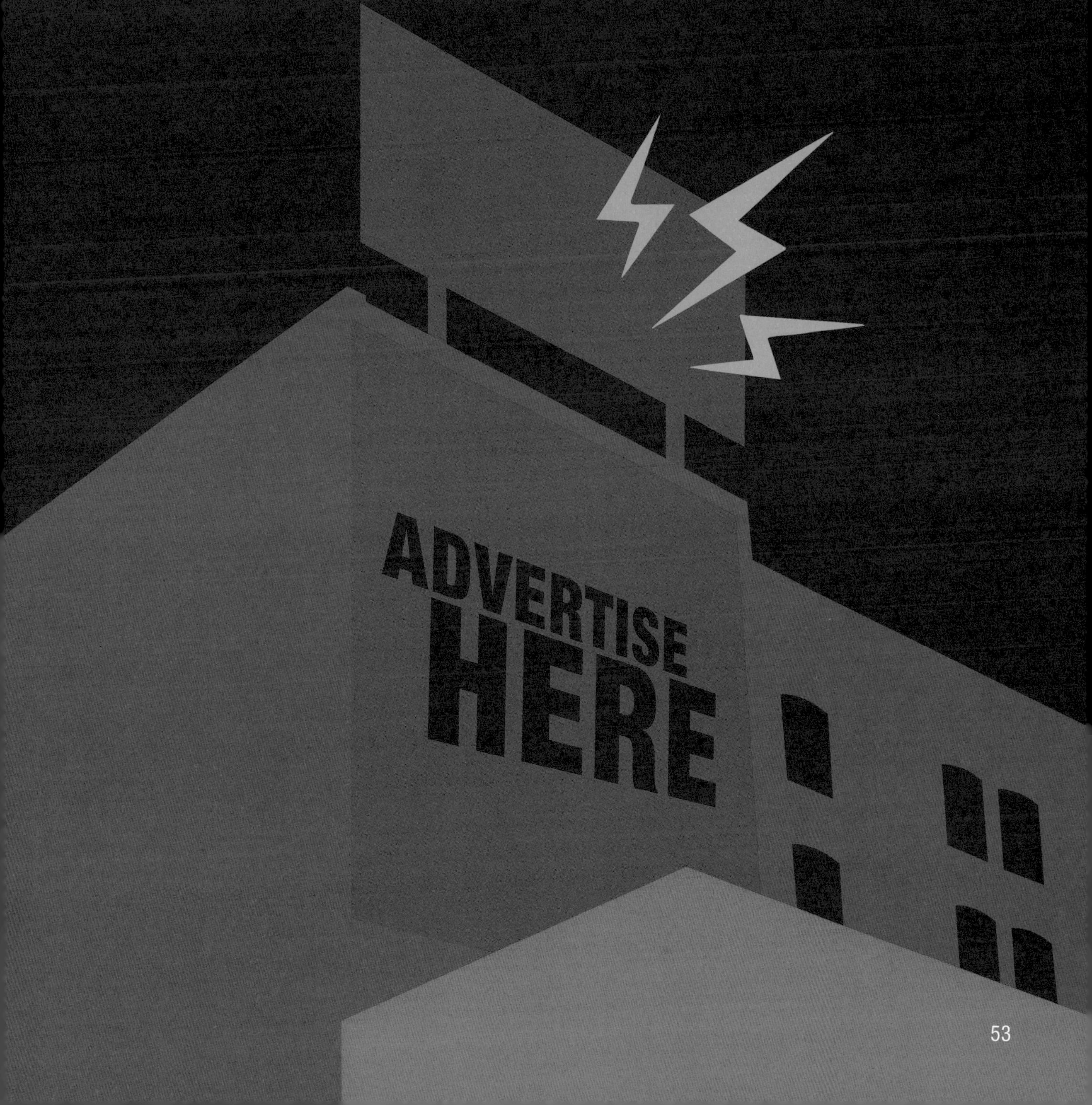
ADVERTISE
HERE

SUMMARY

- Creativity is a Rorschach in language. A capability or feature for engineers, a way of thinking or environment for psychologists, a new experience to evoke human reaction for artists.

- Originality and uniqueness are key in the definition of creativity, though in the domains of arts and technology, we see that true creativity applies new things or interpretations to an end product or experience of value to others.

- The advertising industry has a tension in the definition of creativity, with one camp mainly focusing on originality and difference in a near rebellious way, and another considering that originality needs to be accompanied by some form of value to the end audience.

- When we ask regular people how they describe creative advertising, originality and uniqueness emerge as the most prominent theme, though this is accompanied by a positive experience such as humour, joy and some form of informational value. If we accept the definition of creativity needs to consider the experience of the people advertising needs to influence, from this point, we define it as "an original or different experience that is valued by the end audience".

MISFITS: WHAT WE CAN LEARN FROM THOSE WHO DO NOT FIT IN

What do you think of when you read the word "Misfit"? These words are likely to have a negative connotation, which would not be surprising. Many dictionary definitions are not kind, with one example from Oxford Languages defining a Misfit as *"a person whose behaviour or attitude sets them apart from others in an uncomfortably conspicuous way".* We will start this section by making the case for why this definition is not a wholly accurate one, that it reflects our culture of conformity and how it blinds us to the possibilities of gaining inspiration from such people in the pursuit of creating effective advertising.

Let us deconstruct the Oxford Languages definition. The start is a neutral description, "*a person whose*

behaviour or attitude sets them apart from others". If you are a Misfit, you do not fit in, and being set apart from others is a reasonable description of the word. The latter part though brings forth undertones of the culture of conformity in the education and corporate system we observed earlier, with the words "uncomfortable" and "conspicuous". This part of the definition denotes the perception and reaction of *other people* who are made uncomfortable by them being different. Which brings uncertainty and, as we know, people's brains are wired to reduce uncertainty in their lives.

While this definition likely represents the reaction of most people to Misfits, it misses the value they bring to others by doing the very thing we are wired to avoid: embracing uncertainty. Moving beyond the

misfit noun

dictionary definition, in *The Misfits Manifesto* Lidia Yuknavitch proposes a deeper, more nuanced one that reflects the potential and value Misfits bring to the world:

"*People who think differently are critical to the future of human society. The edges of culture are exactly where new and beautiful meanings are generated. History is made by the Misfits*"[26]

By referring to "*people who think differently*", Yuknavitch makes us think differently about what Misfits are. They are not necessarily different people per se in terms of their appearance or mannerisms, though they sometimes can be. They are people like you and me, albeit with one difference: they think differently. And by thinking differently, they do something very difficult; they embrace *not fitting in* by questioning their assumptions of past experiences. They are comfortable with uncertainty and, in holding this mindset, can see new and original things that have the potential to deliver more value.

If we move beyond the negative stereotype of a Misfit and people being uncomfortable around them, how does this ability to think differently and embrace uncertainty tangibly manifest itself in end value? Also, what is it that we can learn from this in terms of creativity in advertising? Let us turn to some examples of Misfits in culture to understand more about how they think differently and what this means in the process of delivering something *original or different that is valued by the end audience.*

a person whose behaviour or attitude sets them apart from others in an uncomfortably conspicuous way

TONY HAWK

Be a master experimenter

Professional skateboarding is estimated to be a $2BN industry and as of the Tokyo 2020 Games is a recognised Olympic sport[27], but it wasn't always this way.

When starting out in the 1980s, Tony Hawk, now the most famous and wealthy professional skateboarder in the world, and the first to execute a full 900° trick, reflected in a Talks at Google appearance about how his early adoption of skateboarding marked him a target for bullying:

"People don't understand how truly uncool skateboarding was in the early '80s. If you did it, you were instantly marked as an outcast"[28].

Yet despite this negative experience, he was drawn to the creativity of skateboarding, considering it an opportunity to learn and define his own style:

"Skateboarding is highly creative. To be a skater you've got to figure out how to make it your art form. It's not just a sport about who's fastest, who jumps the highest"[28].

And to Hawk, the opportunity to learn was enabled by experimentation. He accepted that he would need to, often at risk to his physical well-being, be open to mistakes and failures, saying that *"A lot of times a mistake will be a beautiful accident"[28].*

Here we see someone, a self-confessed outcast, trying new approaches over and over again, knowing most would not work, though still recognising that the process of experimentation was the best way to learn his craft.

This process is quite different from the traditionally assumed essence of creativity, that it comes from talent or inherent genius. Of course, some talent and quality will need to be evident, but is it alone enough? Or is Hawk overemphasising a need to experiment, when his special talent for riding a skateboard is there for all to see?

In his book *Originals*, Organisational Psychologist, Adam Grant, makes an astute observation about some well-known musical composers, considered to be the most talented in history: Mozart; Beethoven and Bach. Between them, they are considered by musical experts to have created a handful of masterworks. However, to get to these achievements, Mozart composed more than 600 pieces, Beethoven 650 and Bach over a thousand[29]. The point being that, in addition to their raw talent, just like Hawk, these "genius" composers were also master experimenters who were constantly testing and learning different techniques and compositions to reach the pinnacle of their art.

Drawing from these examples and Hawk's experiences in becoming the figurehead for what skateboarding has become today, we come back to advertising. If creativity can contribute to advertising that delivers

stronger business effects, it appears that, like the art form of skateboarding and music, there needs to be an acceptance to invest the time and resources to experiment with a range of directions to learn and get to the best possible outcome. That, ironically, a focus on experimenting and the process to reach excellence in your craft can often lead to more effective outcomes than focusing on the outcome alone. But as we have seen, corporate officers and marketers are people, and peoples' brains are pre-wired to reduce uncertainty.

This brings us back to making our decisions based on assumptions from past experiences. If we pivot the mindset of experimentation from success and failure to an *opportunity to learn*, this can perhaps assuage the craving for certainty, given that the stakes are lower.

In many respects, this is a dynamic we observe in the work we do at Ipsos. We will often start with a brief to help measure the potential effects of directions A, B and C for the advertiser to select one and, based on objective observation of the effects and the identified areas for optimisation, the creative agency identifies a secret direction D, often to the end benefit of the business effects for the advertiser. We will expand on our measurement principles and relationship with end business effects in the next section.

In the meantime, let us return to a simple fact. Tony Hawk is a Misfit. He is a master experimenter, a figurehead of an industry that went from "uncool" to a mainstream $2B annual market value and has a net worth of $140M[30].

SHIGERU MIYAMOTO

Balance the new with the familiar and constantly evolve

Nintendo is one of the world's most successful video console and game developers, with a market cap of $71.2B and a legion of dedicated fans. Much of this success is attributed to lead game designer Shigeru Miyamoto. Originally hired to help design toys, Miyamoto later became responsible for some of the first arcade cabinet games developed in Nintendo, such as Donkey Kong, and the creation of some of its most valuable characters such as Super Mario, the company mascot.

Although Miyamoto's achievements are significant and varied, it is his work with Takashi Tezuka and other game directors on *The Legend of Zelda* that provides a particularly interesting example of what originality really means in creativity. *The Legend of Zelda* game series is set in the mythical land of Hyrule. Here, the player takes control of the protagonist, Link, and his central task is to help or rescue Princess Zelda and defeat the evil wizard, Ganon, and his forces. So far, so familiar. Have we not seen this story before? There are countless classical fairy tales involving princesses, such as Sleeping Beauty and Cinderella. So why can *The Legend of Zelda* be considered to be an original or different experience that is valued?

The key to this answer lies in the gaming experience itself and Miyamoto's openness to connect it to a

familiar story. The first *The Legend of Zelda* game was tasked with providing a follow up title to the launch hit of Super Mario Bros. for the Famicom, or Nintendo Entertainment System (NES) as it is known outside of Japan. To do so, Miyamoto started with his own experiences and observations in childhood.

Growing up in a rural part of Japan called Sonobe, he often explored surrounding forests and was intrigued by what he might find in their darkest corners. It was this intrigue for exploration that he wanted to represent in the gaming experience, which, in turn, acted as the genesis of a new free roaming experience for the player. At the time, most games were left to right side scrolling and very linear in nature. Miyamoto recognised that players should be given the freedom to explore the world around them, finding secrets as the story progressed.

Such a departure from established linear games was rumoured to have made senior Nintendo management nervous about the playing experience and potential sales, as players could get lost in the expanse of the game. Miyamoto though held firm in the belief it was the right direction for the game and the market[31].

He was also able to reassure his colleagues that the game itself was not completely new, that the story was familiar territory and drew from well-known references, such as popular Disney adapted fairy tales.

The commercial success justified the decision-making, with the game becoming one of the biggest sellers for the Famicom/NES, shipping 6.51M units worldwide[32]. Here we see an example of introducing a genuinely new experience to the market, though one that is wrapped in the familiar, be that personal childhood experiences or fairy tales.

This is worth considering when we think about what "originality" actually means. When we hear the word "original", we tend to think of something that has never been seen before. And in some respects, people may perceive the "original" thing in this way, though many creators will openly admit that when they make something original it is based on something else that already exists that they have re-applied in a new way, or they have combined different existing things together in a new way. We can see many other examples of this type in popular movie franchises, such as *Star Wars*. The first movie, *Star Wars: A New Hope (Episode IV)*, was a new experience in many respects when it was released in 1977, combining cutting edge visual effects and orchestral music, set against the vastness of space in a different galaxy. But it was also underpinned by familiar tales of wizards and journeys such as Tolkien's *The Lord of the Rings* and the popular science fiction TV series, Flash Gordon.

FIGURE 9: THE LEGEND OF ZELDA - REPEAT OR EVOLUTION?

REPEAT   **EVOLUTION**

R

The Legend of Zelda

One of the first open world top down gaming experiences

R

Zelda II: The Adventure of Link

Reverts to a left to right side scrolling experience well known in the market

E

TLOZ: A Link to the Past

Moves back to top down free roam, and introduces time travel between parallel worlds

R

TLOZ: Link's Awakening

Continues with top down free roam

E

TLOZ: Ocarina of Time

New 3D game engine and "Z targeting" function to fight enemies

R

TLOZ: Majora's Mask

Same 3D engine. Released near end of N64 lifecycle with Gamecube release pending in 2001

E

TLOZ: The Wind Waker

New animation style and storytelling using a boat to travel between islands

E

TLOZ: Twilight Princess

New Wii motion controls

R

TLOZ: Skyward Sword

Same motion controls

E

TLOZ: Breath of the Wild

More expansive 3D free roaming world, more endurance challenges and expansive secrets

The Legend of Zelda game series also points to the value of evolution in producing enjoyed and commercially successful work. If we count only the games in Canon*, there have been a total of 10 Zelda games published by Nintendo. Each has their own development story, though, for the sake of brevity, the preceding page provides a timeline which summarises the game playing features and classifies each game as being a simple "Repeat" of a previous Zelda game experience or using features from other games, or one that introduces genuinely new gaming experience features and can be considered an "Evolution" of the series.

If we plot the unit sales of each game as a ratio of the consoles available at the time of the game's release[33], representing the available audience at that time, a pattern emerges. The games representing an "evolution" of the Zelda experience nearly always achieved an increase in sales vs. the previous game, while the "repeat" games tend to represent a decrease.

There is though one exception, The Legend of Zelda: Twilight Princess. While we're at risk of confirmation bias in explaining this exception, one reason for it could be the strong focus on the new motion controls in the Wii console, which were not universally well received by gamers, with some finding them clunky and a feature that inhibited their ability to progress in the game. In some respects, this is an example of technical "originality" for originality's sake, without some form of incremental end value in terms of an enjoyable gaming experience.

Irrespective of this one example, we do see a noteworthy trend that there is value in evolution in the creation of content people will pay to experience. To take what you already have and evolve it over time, giving an audience a familiar experience with points of evolution and difference each time. If we turn our attention back to Star Wars, we see another example of the value of evolution, and the consequences of what can happen when you stick to a single formula without introducing new points of difference in the experience.

Star Wars is an iconic and successful movie and entertainment franchise. Loved by millions of people around the world, adults, and children alike, so much so that The Walt Disney Company acquired its makers Lucasfilm Ltd. for $4.05BN[34]. When adjusted for inflation to 2021 levels, the nine films in the

FIGURE 10: +/- % GAME UNIT SALES VS. LAST GAME AS PROPORTION OF TOTAL CONSOLES

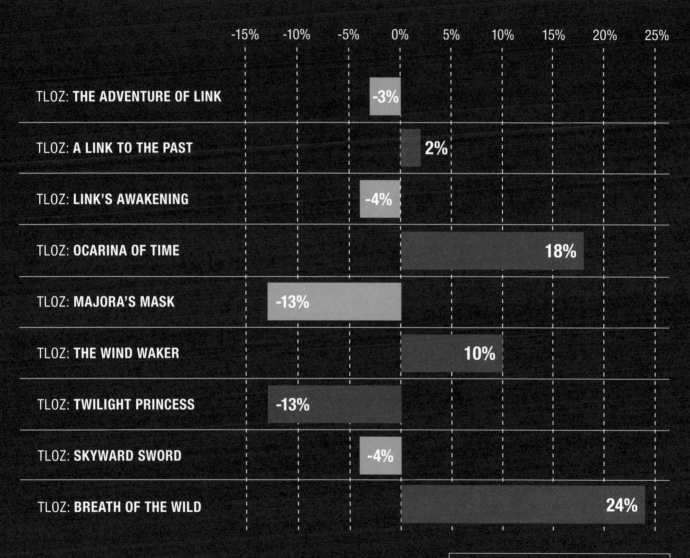

Source: Fandom.com & ign.com - Appendix, Table 1

FIGURE 11: STAR WARS TIMELINE

The Phantom Menace
(1999)

Attack of the Clones
(2002)

Revenge of the Sith
(2005)

A New Hope
(1977)

The Empire Strikes Back
(1980)

Return of the Jedi
(1983)

The Force Awakens
(2015)

The Last Jedi
(2017)

The Rise of Skywalker
(2019)

franchise have grossed close to $15B[35] and formed the intellectual property of toys, merchandise, video games and theme park experiences, delivering even more value and profit.

Since the original trilogy in 1977-1983, another six films have been released, completing what is known in Canon as *The Skywalker Saga*. Although these films have generated incredible financial value, we do see differing levels of success between them and the approach they take in continuing the *Star Wars* story and experience for audiences.

The last six films in the franchise form two separate trilogies; the prequels in Episodes I-III and the sequels in Episodes VII-IX, with each appearing on either side of the originals released in 1977-1983, Episodes IV-VI.

If we review the subsequent trilogies in terms of their financial success at the box office, adjusted for 2021 inflation, the sequels can be considered more successful than the prequels, grossing $4.8BN compared to $3.8BN[35]. However, this does mask a difference in their performance on a metric of absolute importance to Hollywood executives, the rise or drop in takings between films in a franchise.

The reason Hollywood is so enamoured with franchises is because they provide a greater likelihood of box office takings than creating a movie from original source material. When we consider the rise or drop in takings between films in a series of three over the past 30 years, the average difference between a first and second movie is +49% in takings and the difference between the second and third is +9%. This means that if you find an audience with a first film, on average, you will increase your audience and takings in the second and third.

The *Star Wars* prequels and sequels are however different from the average. In each trilogy, the second film takes less at the box office than the first, with a similar decrease of -41% and -38%. They do however diverge in the takings between the second and the third film, with the prequels increasing by +19% and the sequels decreasing by a further -30%.

Why might these two trilogies in a franchise have performed differently with audiences as they progressed, and specifically why did *Episode III: Revenge of the Sith* manage to recover in box office takings when *Episode IX: The Rise of Skywalker* continued a downward trajectory? It is difficult and complex to provide a complete answer to this question, as many external factors could have affected box office performance, such as economic conditions, other entertainment events attracting audience attention, and even the weather on opening weekend. Nevertheless, internal factors related to the audience experience delivered across these films can be considered to partially explain their performance, and they rest in how one trilogy evolved the story of the franchise while another largely repeated what was already known.

If we deconstruct the key components of the story in each film by the type of protagonist, villain and overall narrative arc, and then compare them to the original trilogy, it becomes clear that one attempts an evolution of the story and the other rests more on repetition.

When we compare the protagonists and the villains in each subsequent trilogy, we see a number of similarities to the originals. Both the prequels and the sequels chart the progression of a protagonist of mysterious lineage, like the original trilogy. Both have a villain who is a master of the Dark side of the Force. But they diverge with respect to the narrative arc. The prequels provide an evolution of the story, charting the rise and fall of Anakin Skywalker and his transformation to Darth Vader. There is a similar theme of Anakin being tempted by the Dark side of the Force, as his son Luke was, though the overall story is an evolution of the originals.

By comparison, the sequels have more in common narratively with the originals. Both stories centre on a lone Resistance ship pursued by an Empire Armada, both have protagonists of a mysterious lineage that are tempted to the Dark side of the Force, both leave their training mid-point, both are offered the hand of the villain and refuse, and the villain in both trilogies is redeemed. It should be said that the sequels do have points of difference from the originals. An example is the selection of a female protagonist, which was a bold and progressive choice for a previously male dominated cast, though the sequels are narratively similar to the originals. They repeat the narrative of the originals rather than evolving it with points of difference for the audience, blending the familiar experience of *Star Wars* and evolving it with original or different elements of the story. And in the prequels, like with *The Legend of Zelda* game series, we see a connection between taking this approach and value in terms of retaining and growing an audience.

FIGURE 12: STAR WARS TIMELINE

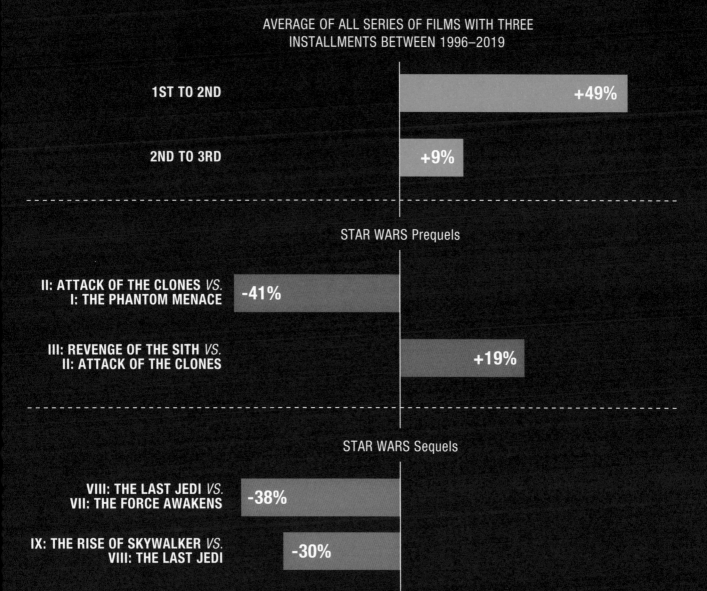

AVERAGE OF ALL SERIES OF FILMS WITH THREE
INSTALLMENTS BETWEEN 1996–2019

1ST TO 2ND +49%

2ND TO 3RD +9%

STAR WARS Prequels

**II: ATTACK OF THE CLONES *VS.*
I: THE PHANTOM MENACE** -41%

**III: REVENGE OF THE SITH *VS.*
II: ATTACK OF THE CLONES** +19%

STAR WARS Sequels

**VIII: THE LAST JEDI *VS.*
VII: THE FORCE AWAKENS** -38%

**IX: THE RISE OF SKYWALKER *VS.*
VIII: THE LAST JEDI** -30%

Source: Appendix, Table 2

ORIGINAL TRILOGY (IV-VI)

PROTAGONIST Luke. A young person of mysterious lineage on a desert planet who goes on an adventure.

VILLAIN Darth Vader. A master of the dark side of the force who wears a mask.

IV: A NEW HOPE

Luke meets Obi-Wan Kenobi. They embark on an adventure to save the galaxy from the Empire. Luke evolves from a young farm hand to a hero of the resistance by destroying the Death Star, and begins to learn the way of the Force.

V: THE EMPIRE STRIKES BACK

Luke is summoned to complete his training and meets Yoda. He leaves his training midway to save his friends and is tempted by visions of the dark side of the Force. Pursued by an armada of enemy ships, the heroes are on the run in a ship. Luke discovers his father is Darth Vader. Vader offers Luke his hand to join him in ruling the galaxy, but he refuses and is defeated by him in a duel, with the consequence of the kidnap of his friend Han Solo.

VI: RETURN OF THE JEDI

Luke becomes a Jedi master and is tempted to the dark side by Darth Sidious. He resists and at near death at the hand of Sidious, Vader sacrifices himself for Luke by killing Sidious, in turn redeeming himself and being one with the light side of the force. Luke and the resistance defeat the Empire and save the Galaxy, and he is joined by the ghosts of the Jedi.

Denotes shared themes in narrative arc to the original trilogy

PREQUEL TRILOGY (I-III)

PROTAGONIST Anakin. *A young person of mysterious lineage,* who we know becomes Darth Vader, but not how.

VILLAIN Darth Sidious. *A master of the dark side of the force.*

I: THE PHANTOM MENACE

Anakin meets Qui-Gon Jin and Obi-Wan Kenobi. They intercept Darth Maul, a Sith Lord, and realise the Sith have returned. Qui-Gon and Obi-Wan are deployed to save the planet of Naboo from occupation by the separatists, where they encounter Darth Maul again. Maul kills Qui-Gon and Obi-Wan kills Maul in return. Obi-Wan commits to train Anakin as his apprentice, setting the first step in his journey to becoming Darth Vader.

II: ATTACK OF THE CLONES

The separatists are at war with the Republic. Anakin is now a young adult and is becoming a powerful Jedi. His mother dies, fuelling him with fear and anger, *tempting him to the dark side of the Force.* Anakin and Padme fall in love and begin a relationship, breaking for Anakin the Jedi code. The Republic defeat the separatists with a clone army and Anakin and Obi-Wan are defeated by a Sith Lord, Count Dooku, as part of the final battle.

III: RETURN OF THE SITH

Padme is pregnant with Anakin's child. He sees visions of her death, further fuelling fear in him. Darth Sidious seduces him to the Dark side of the Force by playing on his fear to save her from death. Anakin kills Jedi master Mace Windu, betraying the Jedi order and becoming Darth Vader. Obi-Wan Kenobi faces Vader and defeats him. Padme and Vader's children, Luke and Leia are born, with Padme dying in labour. They are secretly moved to separate planets to save them from the clutches of Vader and Sidious.

SEQUEL TRILOGY (VII-IX)

PROTAGONIST Rey. *A young person of mysterious lineage on a desert planet who goes on an adventure.*

VILLAIN Kylo Ren. *A master of the dark side of the force who wears a mask.*

VII: THE FORCE AWAKENS

Rey *meets* Finn *and they embark on an adventure to save the galaxy from* the First Order. Rey *evolves from a scavenger to a hero of the resistance by destroying the Death Star and begins to learn the way of the Force.*

Denotes shared themes in narrative arc to the original trilogy

VIII: THE LAST JEDI

Rey finds Luke and he agrees to *help her train to become a Jedi. She leaves her training midway to save her friends and is tempted by visions of the dark side of the Force. The heroes are on the run in a ship, pursued by an armada of enemy ships.* Kylo Ren brings Rey to his master, Snoke, and Snoke asks Ren to kill Rey. *Ren instead kills Snoke. He offers Rey his hand to join him in ruling the galaxy, but she refuses.* Ren has a duel with Luke to discover he has projected himself and the duel was a ruse to allow Rey and the resistance to escape. Rey pilots a ship to lead the resistance to safety and Luke dies.

XI: THE RISE OF SKYWALKER

Darth Sidious returns from the dead, raising a new force of ships and an army of the Sith. Kylo Ren joins Sidious to combine with the First Order to defeat the resistance. Sidious attempts to kill Rey. *Kylo Ren redeems himself by helping Rey to defeat Sidious. Rey and the resistance defeat the Empire and save the Galaxy, and she is joined by the ghosts of the Jedi.*

If we turn back to advertising, we can consider successful campaigns that have followed a similar approach, blending the familiar with the original for a first ad but not stopping there, instead evolving over time with different evolutions to ensure their audience has a familiar, yet different experience for each iteration of the campaign. One campaign that represents this archetype and delivered brand growth is Budweiser *Whassup?*, created in 1999 by DDB Worldwide.

The original campaign took the world by storm and is a textbook example of blending the familiar, a group of friends talking on the phone during a football game, with originality, creating a new language and the now well-known mnemonic of *Whassup?*. In this campaign, we also see a good example of what Feldwick proposes is the value of "popular" advertising; ads that get people talking tend to be effective, represented by an increase of 2.4 million beer barrels shipped in the year after the campaign launched[36]. Moreover, this campaign over time can also be looked at as a fine example of the value of evolution, as it became a series of ads with the most recent iteration in 2020, over 20 years after the original.

After the first ad, the campaign takes the characters from their apartment to a restaurant, a party at another apartment and a live football game in a stadium. All familiar locations until the next ad in the series, where an alien, having infiltrated the human race and observed their behaviour, incidentally by disguising himself as a dog, is asked by his people what he has learned on Earth, to which he, of course, says *Whassup*? A further ad in the series also represents the global phenomenon of the *Whassup?* parlance, with characters in Paris asking *Ça va?*, in Tokyo *Konichiwa*, and characters in Glasgow saying something incomprehensible. All in the spirit of male bonding, brought to you by Budweiser.

Notably, the series did not end there, emerging in its latest incarnation during 2020 and the height of the COVID-19 pandemic. This was a time in the US, and the wider world, of great uncertainty for business and the public alike, with brands in uncoordinated unison producing campaigns that reflected the sombre and concerned state of the day. Each one seemed a near copy of the other, with empty streets, people staring out of windows and brands, all saying they were there for people, in one form or another. While well-intended, this advertising was not very effective, with a majority of campaigns classified as "COVID-style" that Ipsos measured the creative effects of performing below average. There was, however, a notable exception.

FIGURE 13: BUDWEISER "WHASSUP?"

Source: © Budweiser, WHASSUP, 2020[VIII]

The *Whassup?* COVID campaign, created by Anomaly, took a different approach during this troubling time. By updating the original campaign with new voice overs talking about "*being in quarantine*", they provided more light-hearted moments in peoples' lives and deliver end brand effects, represented by being the most effective campaign that referred to COVID-19 that Ipsos measured.

With a first foundation of blending the familiar and the original, we see value in evolution in a campaign, taking the essence of a first successful ad and adding different ingredients over time to deliver a continued positive experience to the end audience, as well as business effects. Much like Miyamoto's approach to *The Legend of Zelda* game series and the *Star Wars* prequels.

Let us return to Miyamoto at this point. Shigeru Miyamoto is a Misfit. He manages to introduce the new alongside the familiar and evolve the gaming experience with new features while retaining key elements that made his games successful. He is Creative Fellow of Nintendo, one of the most successful video game companies in the world.

FIGURE 14: THE SUCCESS OF BUDWEISER'S REVISED "WHASSUP" CAMPAIGN

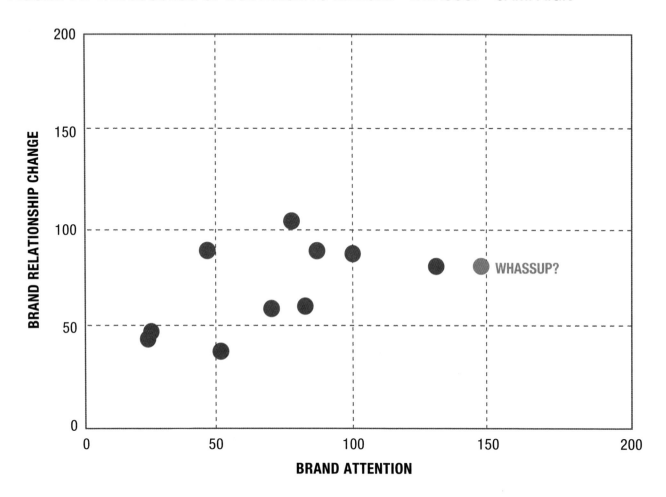

Source: Ipsos

DAVID BOWIE

Look to other things for inspiration and re-apply it

David Bowie is one of the world's most enduring popular icons. Over the course of his career, he is estimated to have sold 140M records[37], making him one of the most commercially successful musical artists of all time. But it is his influence on such a diverse array of musical genres and types of art that represents a more culturally valuable legacy.

His musical influence has crossed folk, rock and pop to the modern day, as well as genres distinct from his own work. An example is the rendition of his song *The Man Who Sold The World* by Nirvana, first recorded in 1970, yet one that became an anthem and synonymous with Seattle grunge music. And his influence has not stopped there, crossing into the world of fashion and inspiring LGBTQ+ artists to more openly express their sexual orientation in their work[38].

This type of varied cultural influence largely stems from his own openness to take inspiration from often disparate areas of art and entertainment. Bowie was, in many respects, a curious, enthusiastic sponge, absorbing ideas and culture around him, learning and reapplying what he experienced. That was to limited commercial success in the short-term, but in the long term, it enabled him to develop a style and music that attracted a large audience and fan base.

Yet Bowie was far from a Misfit in his early music career as Davie Jones. His early work was a near perfect fit into the swinging sixties style of popular Rock 'n' Roll, acting as lead vocalist for The Konrads, Davie Jones & the King Bees and David Jones and the Manish Boys. During this time, Bowie wrote and performed songs with his bands, but the limitation was most of them were inspired by his own life and experiences. Of course, many popular musical artists have found an audience taking this approach, but this did not work for Bowie in finding an audience in the earlier part of his career.

To find his own style and audience, Bowie realised he needed to look *outside* to other forms of art and expression for inspiration. He described this principle in interviews, considering that "*We (musical artists) tend to look at the world as some useable substance, more than a non-artist would*"[39] and that he would do all he could to "*Not be drawn to the tyranny of the mainstream*"[40].

One of the more spurious sources of inspiration he took early in his career was in learning mime, a seemingly illogical time investment for a recording artist. His teacher, Lindsay Kemp, recollected this pursuit was, while different, one of value for Bowie's end live performances:

"*I taught him to exaggerate with his body as well as his voice, and the importance of looking as well as sounding beautiful. Ever since working with me, he's practised that, and in each performance he does, his movements are more exquisite*"[41].

His early commercial successes also drew from the popular culture of the time, with his first commercial hit, *Space Oddity*, melding literal references to the Apollo 11 landing in 1972 and Stanley Kubrick's movie *2001: A Space Odyssey* with his own metaphorical internal struggles finding his place in the world, personified by Ground Control to his Major Tom. The evolution of Major Tom emerged in the first of his characters, Ziggy Stardust, which he used as a vessel for his music in *The Rise and Fall of Ziggy Stardust and the Spiders from Mars.* The character was both other-worldly and androgenous, allowing Bowie to express his bi-sexuality and, in the process, take the first step for LBGTQ+ artists to more openly reference this in their work. The album itself was also Bowie's first commercial success, signifying a culmination of fusing his artistic creativity and re-applying his seemingly questionable time investment in arts such as mime alongside references to science fiction.

The creation of Ziggy also represented the first step on a journey where Bowie would create a character to convey the message of his work, with Aladdin Sane his follow up persona to support the album of the same name. In this incarnation, Bowie was representing his own struggles with stardom, while also reflecting the growing obsession with fame and celebrity in popular culture, with the iconic mark on his face in the album cover depicting the "*crack under the building pressures of a life of fame*"[42].

With his openness to learn and experience from other often unrelated disciplines, we see a key Misfit quality in Bowie. Someone who creates original or different experiences enjoyed by many people not by creating something new per se, but by re-interpreting and re-applying different things in his work.

One of the most famous and long-standing advertising campaigns that benefited from inspiration from the outside is Nescafe Gold Blend "Couple", a series of ads created by McCann Erickson that first ran in the UK between 1987 to 1993. Up until that time, most coffee advertising focused on the taste and aromas of the product, selling to the audience the promise of a high quality and sophisticated experience.

Rather than following this well-set trend, McCann Erikson looked for outside inspiration and popular entertainment to tell a story of how Gold Blend could bring people together. At this time, TV series such as Dallas and Dynasty were capturing the attention of the nation, with tense and smouldering romantic drama, and the "Couple" ads capitalised on this, providing audiences a British experience in a series of 12 Gold Blend TV ads, focusing on two characters, Tony and Sharon, whose relationship develops over time thanks to their love of Gold Blend.

In the first ad, we see Sharon buzzing on Tony's doorbell asking if she can borrow some coffee for a dinner party. Over subsequent ads, they grow closer and are set to go to dinner. Then, like the popular TV dramas of the day, there are moments of tension, when Sharon believes incorrectly Tony is in a relationship with another woman; likewise, Tony makes the same mistake when introduced to her brother. The final ad in the series culminates in Tony telling Sharon he loves

McCann Erikson looked for outside inspiration and to popular entertainment to tell a story of how Gold Blend could bring people together

her, with 30 million people reported to have tuned in to watch what became a cultural event[43]. These ads were not only sought after content from audiences but were also responsible for an impressive sales volume growth of 60% over the time they were aired[44].

Companies other than coffee brands have also looked to outside sources of inspiration when developing their advertising. One such campaign is Apple's "1984", created by Chiat/Day. While home computers and smartphones are now near ubiquitous in the developed world, the 1980s was a decade in which these devices were first being introduced into homes at scale, and while Apple had a passionate following even then, its sales were dwarfed by the then dominant IBM[45].

The battle between the two companies was not quite David and Goliath, but not far from it. Against this backdrop, Chiat/Day looked to popular science fiction to personify the battle Apple had with IBM to win hearts and minds to have their devices adopted

FIGURE 15: NESCAFE GOLD BLEND "COUPLE"

Source: © Nescafé, Gold Blend Couple, 1987-1993[IX]

by more US homes, by borrowing from the dystopian tale of George Orwell's *1984*. Released as a movie starring John Hurt in the same year of its title, Chiat/Day pitched to audiences the status quo of home computing as a grey corporate Big Brother on a screen talking to an audience about "*a garden of pure ideology*" and a "*Unification of Thoughts*". After this, a woman in bright clothing runs towards the screen, hurling a hammer and destroying it. We are then presented with a narrated end text: "*On January 24th, Apple Computer will introduce Macintosh. And you'll see why 1984 won't be like 1984*".

Here we see another example of an agency and brand looking outside their own category conventions of communicating product features and specifications.

FIGURE 16: PERSONAL COMPUTER MARKETSHARE DURING THE 8-BIT ERA (1000S OF UNITS)

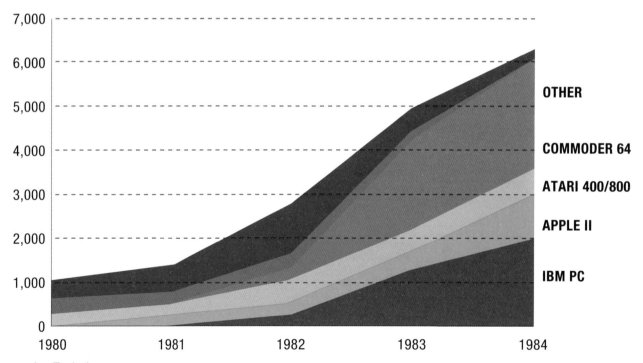

Source: Ars Technica

Instead, they looked to popular science fiction to help them create a story. One of David vs. Goliath, but more than that, uniformity and corporate hegemony against a company in Apple that could inspire individuality and creativity.

At this point, let us return to Bowie, an inarguable creative individual. David Bowie is a Misfit. He is one of the most commercially successful recording artists in music history. He looked to the world around him to experience often divergent and disconnected disciplines and re-applied them to create original and enjoyable music. He remains an iconic inspiration for many people around the world, across music, entertainment, fashion and culture.

FIGURE 17: APPLE "1984"

Source: © Apple, 1984, 1984[x]

SUMMARY

- The definition of a Misfit being someone who is different that makes us uncomfortable is an outdated stereotype. Instead, they are people who think differently and help the wider world by identifying new solutions that add value to their audience.

- Misfits are master experimenters. They get to truly creative work by accepting they need to produce higher volumes than others and positively embrace making mistakes as an opportunity to better learn their craft.

- Misfits connect the new with the familiar and understand they need to evolve their offer over time, building on the foundation of their earlier work.

- Misfits look towards seemingly disconnected work and disciplines for inspiration when creating their own work. They then interpret and re-apply what they see to create original or different experiences that are valued by their end audience.

THE ROLE OF CREATIVITY AND A MISFIT MINDSET IN ADVERTISING EFFECTS

We have described advertising as an investment to achieve end business value in short-term sales and longer term market share gains, but how specifically does it do this, and how can we measure these effects?

In this section, we will review the types of advertising experiences that are linked to end effects and identify where creativity, *an original or different experience that is valued by the end audience*, plays a role in delivering them. Before proceeding further, let us remind ourselves of the target audience of advertising… regular people.

Regular people do not think or care much about most brands and products they buy. In fact, if 75% of the brands available to people disappeared today, they would be easily replaced by another option[46]. This is because brands as entities are not tangible or physical in nature, but a collection of associations and experiences in the minds of the target audience. A memory network of thoughts, images, colours, sounds and stories. They are the product of our past experiences and assumptions. They are in many respects a tool for people to manage uncertainty, to efficiently be as certain as possible that the brand that comes to mind is the best possible choice for the need they have, be that functional, emotional or both. In this context, the role of advertising is to reinforce memories for the advertised brand or disrupt those of competitors, to trigger more deliberate processing, so

that the advertised brand is more likely to be picked up or used at a later point of choice or consumption.

If we accept brands are intangible memories that can be reinforced or disrupted over time, what advertising needs to achieve to deliver business effects is to encode memories linked to the brand that can evoke desire and change end choices and behaviour both in the short and long-term.

Ipsos Creative Excellence has developed proprietary methods to observe these effects of advertising. Firstly, we measure the ability of the advertising to encode memories linked to the brand, measured by Brand Attention. We then measure the effect of the advertising experience to influence short-term choices and longer term perceptions with the Behaviour Change and Brand Relationship metrics. Each of these is combined with Brand Attention to provide a measure of the advertising potential to increase sales in the short-term, defined as a period of 4-6 weeks, via the Creative Effect Index (CEI), as well as longer term market share gains, defined as a period of at least six months, via the Equity Effect Index (EEI). Both end indices have been validated to in market outcomes, Market Mix Modelling for short-term sales and measures of Attitudinal Equity, linked to market share, in brand tracking.

More specifically, we measure the effects of Brand Attention and Behaviour Change using the following techniques.

FIGURE 18: BRAND ATTENTION / BRAND DESIRE

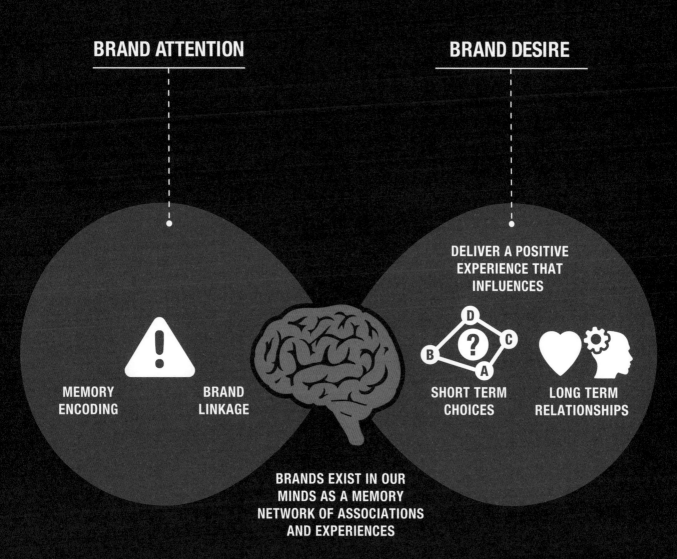

FIGURE 19: CREATIVE EFFECT INDEX – CEI AND INDEXED SALES LIFT

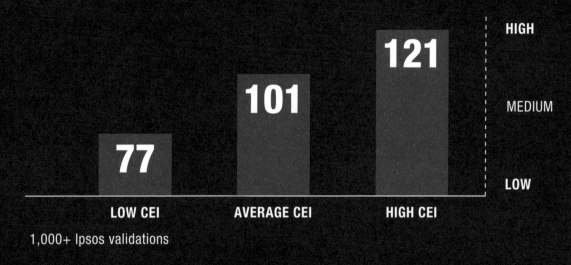

1,000+ Ipsos validations

FIGURE 20: EQUITY EFFECT INDEX – EEI AND LONG TERM MARKET SHARE GAINS

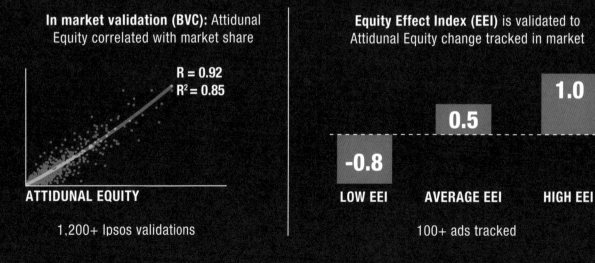

In market validation (BVC): Attidunal Equity correlated with market share

R = 0.92
R² = 0.85

ATTIDUNAL EQUITY

1,200+ Ipsos validations

Equity Effect Index (EEI) is validated to Attidunal Equity change tracked in market

100+ ads tracked

Brand Attention

We measure Brand Attention by exposing people to advertising alongside other advertising and entertainment content. This helps us measure the potential of the advertising to perform "in the wild," alongside other distractions and content. After this distracted exposure where the person is unaware of the advertising of interest to the experiment, we present de-branded stills of the video advertising and ask them if they can remember seeing it. Those who confirm they have encoded the advertising in their minds are also asked an open-ended question to confirm if they can name the advertised brand. These measures are then combined to create Brand Attention.

FIGURE 21: IPSOS BRAND ATTENTION MEASURES

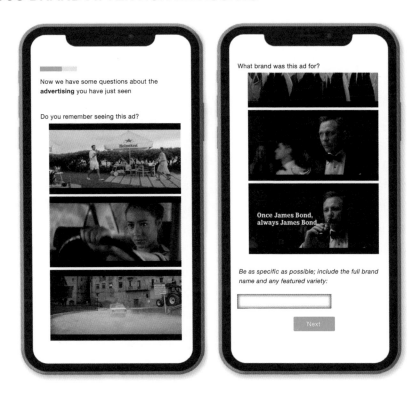

Behaviour Change

We utilise an exposed, unexposed design to measure the effects of the advertising experience on the Thoughts of people, or the likelihood the brand will be chosen. This design is underpinned by Behavioural Science principles, which enables us to measure intuitive effects on the advertised choice, relative to other salient choices in the mind of each individual person.

We take a similar approach to measuring longer term emotional and functional perceptions to calculate Relationship Change, representing the ability of the advertising to strengthen the likelihood that the brand can meet emotional and functional needs and therefore the likelihood is felt to be a good, long term choice.

We contextualise these effects on Thoughts using Neuroscience to measure the immediate Emotions via facial coding and Data Science to measure the valence and intensity of residual Feelings via text analytics of open-end responses. In addition, we ask a range of questions about the perception of the advertising experience people had and compare these responses to normative benchmarks.

By providing this holistic set of measures across Thoughts, Feelings and Emotions, we can advise our clients and their agencies as to which creative directions have the most potential and any areas that can benefit from optimisation, if needed.

Having outlined the techniques we use to measure advertising effects and how they link to end business outcomes, let us now turn to the scope of the analytic exercise we did to understand the role of creativity in achieving them.

FIGURE 22: *CREATIVE / SPARK* DRAWS FROM MULTIPLE SCIENCE DISCIPLINES

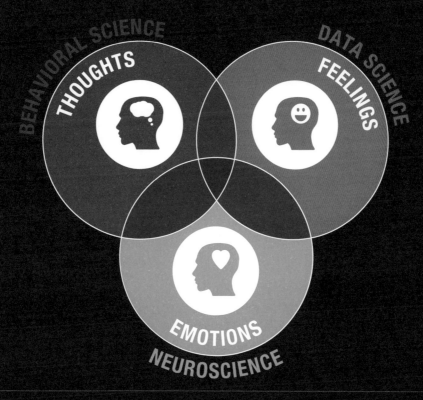

THOUGHTS
The choices we make, based on our past experiences and associations

FEELINGS
The residual, unarticulated feelings that stay with us after an experience

EMOTIONS
The immediate bodily responses we have to stimulus and experiences

Scope of Analysis

Ipsos Creative Excellence has measured the effects of over 200,000 video ads using our proprietary methods. To understand the role of creativity in advertising effects, we reviewed a sample of 13,000 recently evaluated ads and identified a sub-sample of approximately 1,700 cases balanced by category and country for the analysis. Each case was based on at least 150 people, sampled as buyers or intenders in the category of the advertised brand. The cases in the corpus encompassed a range of categories, including food, pet care, beverages, beauty, baby care, tech and media, healthcare and financial services, across 18 countries.

With this robust data set of the core effects of Brand Attention, Behaviour Change and Relationship Change on Thoughts, we related these effects to the experience of the advertising using our standard measures of the perception of the experience people have via a two-step analytic approach:

i. **Classifying the Advertising Experience:** we used factor analysis to connect our standard measures of the advertising experience into different groups of overall experiences. There were a total of 14 specific measures, each asked as a statement that people can use to describe the experience they had. By employing the factor analysis, the groupings were bottom up defined in terms of how they best fit together based on the responses of regular people, rather than top down based on practitioner experience for how arbitrarily we thought they should fit together.

ii. **Relating the Advertising Experiences to Effects:** we created combined factor scores for the experience groups. We then placed these scores of the advertising experiences into a General Linear Regression model to identify the amount of variance each explained for the overall effects measured.

In taking this two-step analytic approach, we wanted to understand two things:

1. Is our proposed definition of creativity in advertising (*an original or different experience that is valued by the end audience*) and the essence of Misfits (*people who do not fit in and achieve more effective outcomes*) represented in the different overall advertising experiences we identified?

2. If creativity does feature in these types of experiences, how, if at all, is it related to advertising effects in the short and long term?

Let us now review the key findings of the analysis and the accompanying implications for the investment in creativity in advertising.

Advertising delivers experiences that harness Creativity and Empathy

The factor analysis identified three advertising experiences, representing an interaction of creativity and empathy.

Each of these experiences is a group of more specific perceptions and experiences of advertising. Some have a higher loading factor in the overall group, represented by a larger size of the bubble, and the presence of one tends to be accompanied by the presence of others in the grouping.

This does not mean that if one overall experience is linked to an ad, the others will not be, nor does it mean that one experience is more related to advertising effects than another. What it does mean is that, based on the responses of regular people to advertising, some specific experiences and perceptions group together more naturally than others. This, in turn, can inform our view of where, if at all, creativity features in the overall advertising experience.

Across these three experiences, we see two that bear a relationship to our earlier definition of creativity in advertising, *an original or different experience that is valued by the end audience*. These are a *Creative Experiences* and *Creative Ideas*, **experiences that do not fit in**.

FIGURE 23: THREE ADVERTISING EXPERIENCES

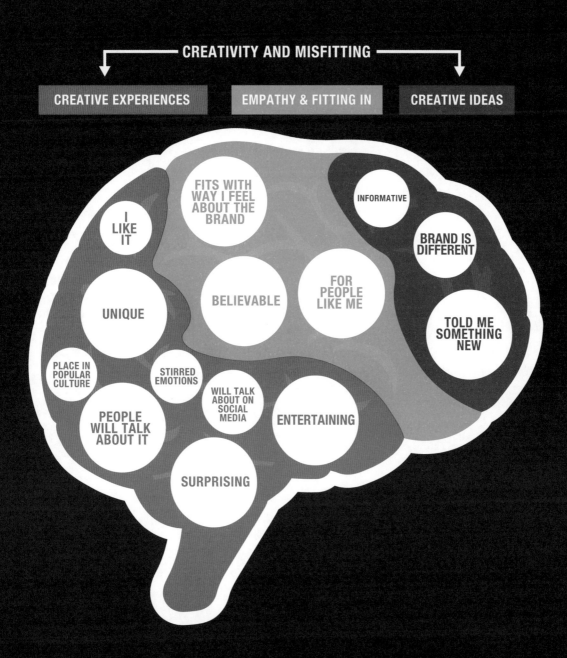

CREATIVE EXPERIENCES: a unique advertising experience that entertains, evokes an emotional response, and is expected to be talked about.

In this grouping, we see clear evidence of the elements of creativity proposed in our definition. One that is *original or different*, represented by "unique" and "surprising", and *is valued in some form by the end audience*, represented by "entertaining", "I liked it" and "stirred my emotions". In this case, the "value" denotes the experience itself, one that is entertaining. Additionally, we see evidence from these groupings that an original and entertaining experience is related to an expectation that "people will talk about it" and "has a place in popular culture", or as Feldwick described in *Why Does the Pedlar Sing?*, something considered to be *"popular"*.

In this grouping, we observe a further signal that difference does not exist as a single entity in terms of an advertising experience, thus supporting the more nuanced definition of creativity represented by Burnett. While it's a further sign of a more complex role of creativity in the experience of advertising than difference alone, we should be clear that this does not mean difference and originality is less important than entertainment. Based on the factor analysis, a belief people had a "unique" or "surprising" experience co-exists with an "entertaining" and "popular" one. These elements are interdependent and tend to be experienced together.

CREATIVE IDEAS: an experience that introduces new ideas and thinking.

In *Creative Ideas*, we see our definition of creativity represented, though rather than the experience, the concepts and ideas are perceived to be "new", and this is also related to an expectation the advertised "brand is different". Here, we see in the advertising experience a potential to introduce new or original ideas, with the possibility to trigger more deliberative thinking and break free from the automatic, familiar and safe. This represents a key quality we have seen from the Misfits of the world, that they are people who propose ideas and solutions that *do not fit in.*

An example of advertising communicating original ideas of value are those that highlight the ways in which people can live more environmentally friendly lives, such as washing their clothes or dishes at a low temperature. This helps them save energy reducing the environmental impact of their household, and the advertised product happens to be part of the ideas communicated, but it is not the focal point of attention.

Creative Ideas, as well as a *Creative Experience*, provide evidence that some advertising leverages the elements of creativity we have identified, by delivering an experience that does *not* fit in, alongside the value of entertainment. While these experiences are evident, we now need to understand if they are in any way related to end advertising effects. Before we do this, let us first consider another advertising experience that emerged in the factor analysis, less borne of creativity, and not fitting in, and more of empathy and fitting with what is known. As stated before, people are pre-wired to manage and reduce uncertainty in their lives, often gravitating to the safe and familiar choices they have made before. And here we see another advertising experience that meets this very human need.

Empathy & fitting in

While creativity features in the experiences reviewed so far, this is balanced with one of Empathy, where *things fit.* An experience less of difference, originality, and entertainment and more of the familiar and known, anchored in human empathy, and reflecting the world as the target audience knows it. This is represented by the perception the advertising is "for people like me", that it is relatable and has some connection with what is already known or in some form has been experienced. Fitting the belief the advertising is aimed at them. This experience also includes a perception that it "fits with the way I feel about this brand". Here we see an advertising experience meeting the previously-explored need for certainty and familiarity for people. This could be a consistent creative style or message from previous campaigns, or at a more tactical level, the use of Distinctive Brand Assets, originally defined by Byron Sharp and Jenni Romaniuk of the Ehrenberg-Bass Institute as "the non-brand name elements that trigger the brand into the memory of category buyers"[47].

Alongside the feeling the advertising fits what is known about the brand and represents the target audience is the perception that events in the advertising are "believable". By "believable", we need to accept that different ads may evoke different responses in terms of the idea or overall experience being credibly connected to the brand, or what is shown is more generally accepted as possible. Regardless, there is little doubt

this grouping represents less creativity and difference and more an experience where things fit what is known, as if you believe the ideas or what you have seen, you will have some form of reference point from the past to inform this.

Across these overall types of advertising experiences, we then see the more nuanced definition of creativity represented by *Creative Experiences*, via a grouping of attributes, "unique", "surprising", "entertaining", having a "place in popular culture", an expectation others "will talk about it", and a core quality of a Misfit mindset, Creative Ideas, via being presented with something "new". As a counterbalance, we have also identified an experience that represents *Empathy and Fitting In*. The perception the advertising depicts "believable" events that are "for people like me", and "fits" with expectations of the brand. In essence, an experience that "fits" prior expectations and the world around the target audience.

Having defined these experiences representing creativity and empathy in advertising, we now need to understand to what extent, if at all, they are related to advertising effects both in the short and long term. What role, if any, does creativity play in advertising effects, and what does this mean for making the case for creativity in the boardroom, to reassure and reduce uncertainty when investing in the production of advertising?

CREATIVITY MATTERS IN ADVERTISING

After placing the different experience groups into the regression model and relating them to key advertising effects, we identified clear evidence that creativity matters, in the short and long term.

Creative Experiences had the strongest relationship with Memory Encoding, the effect where the advertising experience has been stored in memory to later have the possibility to influence choices and end behaviour.

We observed that *Creative Ideas* have a relationship with short term effects, at similar levels to *Empathy and Fitting In*, representing the importance of *both* types of experiences in influencing short-term choices. Both experiences also had the strongest relationship with longer term relationship effects, though *Creative Ideas* was slightly stronger.

Having mapped the relationship between these three advertising experiences and end creative effects, we see evidence that creativity matters in advertising. *Creative Experiences* is the most important factor in

encoding the advertising in memory. Also, *Creative Ideas* play a significant role in advertising being effective at influencing brand choices in the short-term and relationships in the longer term.

But creativity is not solely responsible for explaining advertising effects. Experiences that draw on empathy, reflect the world of the target audience, provide familiarity, and fit into what is already known or expected, are also important.

In these relationships, we see an interplay between creativity and *not fitting in* and empathy and *fitting in*. This suggests that difference alone is unlikely to deliver strong advertising effects; instead, they need to interconnect with the relatable and familiar in some way. But why might this interplay be present and what does this mean for how agencies and advertisers can apply creativity in advertising? We will now outline these relationships further with key data points, propose why they might exist and how brands and agencies can learn to harness them to get to successful business outcomes.

FIGURE 24: RELATIONSHIPS BETWEEN ADVERTISING EXPERIENCES AND EFFECTS

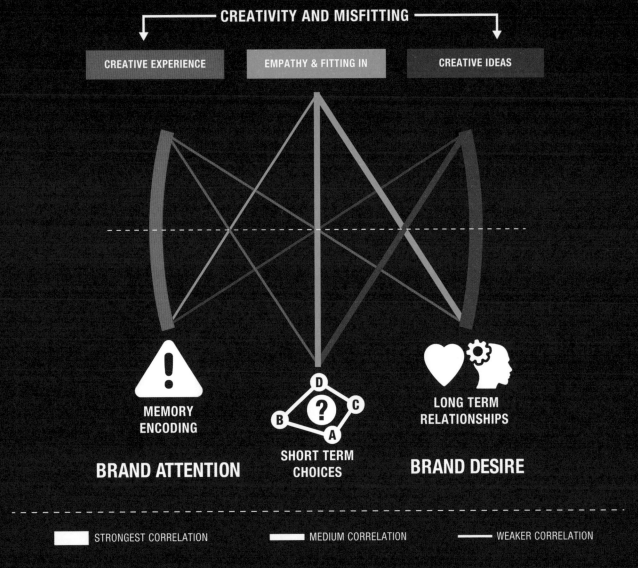

Source: Linear Regression Model of the relationship between Advertising Experience Types and Evaluative Metrics from Ipsos Global Creative Evaluation Database (n=1,734 cases)

Memory Encoding and Creative Experiences

If brands are a collection of memories and experiences in our minds, then the role of effective advertising is to be encoded in the mind, to reinforce or create new memories to the benefit of the advertised brand. Think of this as the price of admission, to have an opportunity to influence the likelihood your brand is chosen over others. If the advertising is not even attended to and encoded in memory, the chances of this happening are very low.

In the analysis, we observe that *Creative Experiences*, those that are "unique", "surprising", "entertaining", "emotional", "has a place in popular culture" and are expected to be "talked about", have the strongest relationship with Memory Encoding.

Why might this be the case? That if people have an advertising experience they have not seen before, that entertains them and they expect other people will talk about it, why are they more likely to remember it?

One explanation is reflected in the Misfits and advertising campaigns we reviewed earlier. Campaigns such as Nescafe Gold Blend "Couples" and Budweiser "Whassup" were certainly considered different for the time, introducing sequential ad storytelling or a new language, and they also, like David Bowie, took inspiration from outside, from other parts of popular culture. This relationship also supports Feldwick's proposal in *Why Does the Pedlar Sing?* that effective advertising is "a performance", one that entertains and has some expectation it is popular.

At this point, we can turn to another campaign that we believe embodies unique and entertainment principles, and it comes from Heineken, who we saw earlier make strong efforts to embed creativity into the DNA of their advertising. This specific campaign was first aired in 2019 for their Heineken green bottle beer brand and is an example of how advertising can meld the world of entertainment and brands to great effect.

FIGURE 25: ADS THAT DELIVER A CREATIVE EXPERIENCE ARE MOST LIKELY TO BE ENCODED IN MEMORY

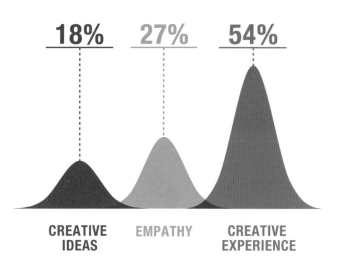

% PROPORTION OF VARIANCE EXPLAINED IN REGRESSION MODEL FOR MEMORY ENCODING

Source: Ipsos Global Creative Evaluation Database (n=1,734 cases)

FIGURE 26: ADS THAT DELIVER A CREATIVE EXPERIENCE ARE MOST LIKELY TO BE ENCODED IN MEMORY – USA CASE LEVEL DATA

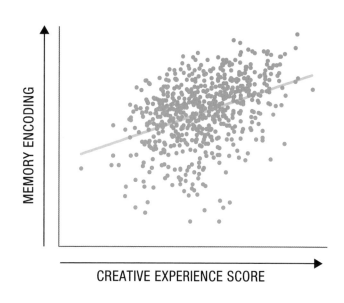

Source: Ipsos USA Creative Evaluation Database (n=647 cases)

FIGURE 27: HEINEKEN "JAMES BOND"

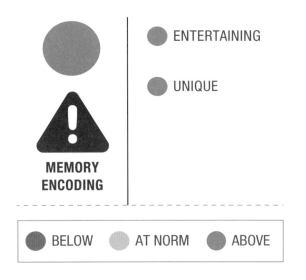

ENTERTAINING

UNIQUE

MEMORY ENCODING

BELOW   AT NORM   ABOVE

In the campaign, Daniel Craig, the actor who plays James Bond, is on a relaxing holiday and gets in a taxi. When he gets out of the taxi, he realises he has left his passport on the passenger seat and what ensues is a chase to retrieve the said passport from his taxi driver. The chase includes several humorous moments where Craig is assumed to be James Bond, but his behaviour, including the drinking of a Heineken beer rather than Bond's Vodka Martini, is contrary to this expectation.

This creative device delivers a Memory Encoding effect above the norm, along with an above norm experience that is "entertaining" and "unique". In many respects, this campaign is the archetypal "performance" that is as much content that entertains as it is advertising to promote and grow a brand. And Heineken is far from alone in taking the role of an entertainer delivering a performance, rather than a brand pitching a product to the doorstep of the mind.

Laundry detergent is not in the consciousness of most people. By its nature, it is a very functional, commoditised category and, if it works well, its effects on cleaning clothes are not visible. This category dynamic poses a challenge if you are the market leader, as Tide is in the United States.

Faced with this challenge, P&G looked to creativity and their agency Saatchi & Saatchi to produce a campaign to defend their market position. The result was their now famous "It's a Tide Ad" campaign, which was founded on the idea that if most laundry advertising focuses on dirt and stains, they should not fit in by talking about cleanliness.

Launched at the 2018 SuperBowl, it beautifully blurred the line between entertainment and advertising by making viewers think any ad could be "a Tide Ad", and it did so by turning the stereotypical tropes of advertising on its head. In the launch ad, the spokesperson, David Harbour, is shown in a series of scenes depicting "typical" advertising. It opens

FIGURE 28: HEINEKEN "JAMES BOND"

Source: © Heineken, James Bond, 2020[XI]

with Harbour driving a premium yet indistinct car in a smart suit, which transitions to him in a bar with a group of young people in a "hilarious" beer ad, then to a diamond ad, a soft drink ad with young attractive people on the beach, and so on. Every ad is a "Tide Ad", as the clothes are clean and this could only have been delivered by Tide.

This launch ad is in many respects a totem of a Creative Experience. It is undoubtedly unique, it entertains and is talkable. That it achieves this experience by overtly calling out stereotypes and category codes in advertising is also interesting, that it recognises audiences not only non-consciously screen out these ads, but they are also consciously a source of ridicule and humour that can act as a vehicle for Tide to stand out and own the conversation at the SuperBowl.

The advertising experience also did not stop at the launch ad. More executions hijacking advertising stereotypes were intermittently peppered into the ad breaks to keep people guessing if the next ad was a "Tide Ad". Examples also included hijacks of P&G's own brands, such as Old Spice and Mr Clean, further blurring the lines between Tide and other ads.

The results for P&G were as impressive as they were entertaining. In their Effie award submission, P&G reported high volumes of social conversation and earned media value, as well as, most importantly, a sales increase subsequent to the SuperBowl campaign. Such was the effectiveness of this campaign that it won a Global Grand at the Effie Global Best of the Best Awards. Across the earned media, sales increase and award recognition. This campaign then represents an example of how taking a mindset of not fitting in and focusing on entertaining your audience can lead to tangible business outcomes.

We observed in our analysis that another key element of *Creative Experiences* is evoking an emotional response, in this case, the agreement that the advertising experience "stirred your emotions". Outside this observation of the role of emotion in Memory Encoding effects in advertising, it has also been observed in a range of academic studies that emotional responses influence attention[48], perception[49] and memory encoding (encoding, storage, and retrieval of information)[50, 51].

But what exactly is emotion and why does it have a role in Memory Encoding effects in advertising? While there is a range of definitions of what an emotion is, with many referring to "instinct" and "intuition", Ipsos subscribes to the one proposed by Davidson, "*a relatively brief episode of coordinated brain, autonomic and behavioural changes that facilitate a response to an event of significance for the organism*"[52].

FIGURE 29: P&G/TIDE "IT'S A TIDE AD"

Source: © P&G, Strangely Noticeable, 2020[XII]

With immediacy key and neither the brain nor the body the sole emitter of emotional responses, we can consider that the perception of an emotional experience, the agreement that the ad "stirred my emotions" does not measure the exact experience advertising needs to deliver. People can have an opinion on their recollection of the experience being an emotional one that, on one level, is perfectly valid, though it may misrepresent the immediacy of the advertising experience and over or under-represent the role of emotion in influencing end advertising effects.

This is why at Ipsos we measure a combination of Thoughts, Feelings *and* Emotions when measuring advertising effects. As mentioned before, in the case of emotion, we integrate facial coding as standard in our solutions, meaning we can measure an immediate emotional response and link this to the effect of advertising on Thoughts, such as Memory Encoding and Brand Attention.

Figure 30 shows an analysis to understand if there is such a relationship between a positive immediate emotional response and creative effects, where we averaged the second-by-second response across n=734 ads and compared the top to the bottom performers on Brand Attention.[52]

Here we see that ads that perform strongest on Brand Attention overall are more likely to elicit a positive emotional experience that grows over time and finishes

FIGURE 30: AVERAGE POSITIVE EMOTIONAL RESPONSE OVER TIME BY BRAND ATTENTION PERFORMANCE

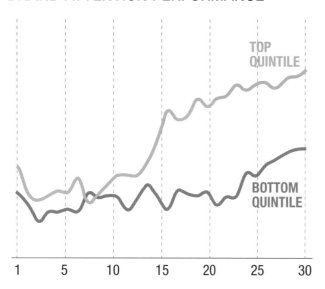

on a high. The arc of the emotional response over time for the top performing ads also conforms to the Fredrickson and Kahneman "Peak end rule", where they observed differences in the memory of an experience overall based on how it was manipulated at the end.[54]

What we can consider from these relationships is that, in addition to an entertaining and unique experience, eliciting a positive emotional response that finishes on a high is also important in maximising the likelihood that an ad is encoded in memory. If they had a positive experience when viewing the ad, their brain is more likely to encode some of this experience in memory given that there is a non-conscious hope the positive experience could be repeated.

Another example of a campaign that evokes emotion via entertainment is Hello toothpaste. A lesser-known brand in the Colgate Palmolive portfolio, Hello uses natural ingredients to provide fresh clean breath and an enjoyable tooth brushing experience. On the surface of this description, there is not much here that is creative. Also, toothpaste could be considered a difficult category to gain sales and share in because it is a ubiquitously used product with large dominating brands.

Enter the "Strangely Noticeable" ad, that took a different approach to the established norms of toothpaste campaigns, focusing on science and whiter than white teeth. The ad shows people using the product. However, instead of focusing on the outcome, it showcases the *experience* of using it, with people brushing and then taking a moment to pause to realise how much they enjoy it. The ad culminates in a moment where one of the characters is so surprised she says "Holy S#*t!".

FIGURE 31: HELLO "STRANGELY NOTICEABLE"

Source: © Hello, Strangely Noticeable, 2020[XIII]

With this ad, we then see an alternative to an approach to investing in a big production with a star actor and instead using simple yet effective humour to convey a unique or different experience that people could participate in. As a result, this ad delivers a *Creative Experience* that is strongly encoded in memory. With an above norm agreement it is "entertaining", "unique", "surprising", and delivers a positive emotional experience that finishes high, leaving the audience wanting more.

Let us now turn to another critical effect advertising needs to achieve when memories are encoded in the mind, that they need to be linked to the advertised brand. In this analysis, we observed there is not a creative experience you can deliver that can improve your chances of this happening. But fear not, there is clear evidence that the brand assets you use in your experience are important to achieve this.

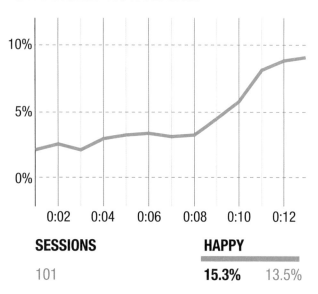

FIGURE 32: HELLO
"STRANGELY NOTICEABLE"

SESSIONS
101

HAPPY
15.3%   13.5%

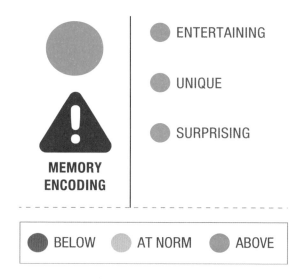

FIGURE 33: HELLO
"STRANGELY NOTICEABLE"

ENTERTAINING

UNIQUE

SURPRISING

MEMORY
ENCODING

BELOW   AT NORM   ABOVE

Distinctive Brand Assets Fuel Brand Attention

Memory Encoding is only one effect advertising needs to achieve to have an opportunity to influence choices and behaviour. If the brand is not linked to the encoded memories, it is for nought, and even has the potential to positively influence your competitors, depending on the category you compete within for market share.

This brings us to the outcome of the regression analysis for Brand Linkage, the ability of the advertising to encode and connect the brand name to any memories. We observed a weak relationship across all experience types, with a positive co-efficient less than R=0.1. This would suggest there is no experience as such that can ensure your brand features in the encoded memories of the advertising. You can entertain and deliver an original experience that includes new and different ideas, but this will not guarantee the brand will be remembered. So, what does this mean for creativity and its role in enabling Brand Attention? While no singular experience can amplify the chances of your brand being encoded in memory, we know from the evidence of other Ipsos analysis that the use of Distinctive Brand Assets, "the non-brand name elements that trigger the brand into the memory of category buyers"[47], has a significant role to play.

The assets some brands have at their disposal to encode the brand more easily in peoples' minds are cues and signals leveraging non-verbal based stimuli, such as visual colours, logos, characters, celebrities, audio devices and music, scents/tastes when using the brand or product. To better understand the value of such assets to advertising effects, we classified approximately 2,000 video ads we had evaluated based on presence, frequency and the length of time assets were featured. We then compared the ads that used assets with those that did not to understand the relationship with Brand Attention effects.

In this exercise, we observed there is a relationship between the use of assets and Brand Attention, with ads placed in the top third of the database found to have used +52% more brand assets on average than low performers[55]. Interestingly, there was little difference between the high and low performers on the frequency of saying or showing the brand name, further suggesting the power of visual and auditory brand cues, in enabling advertisers to weave their brand into the advertising experience more seamlessly.

FIGURE 34: RELATIONSHIP BETWEEN THE USE OF ASSETS AND BRAND ATTENTION

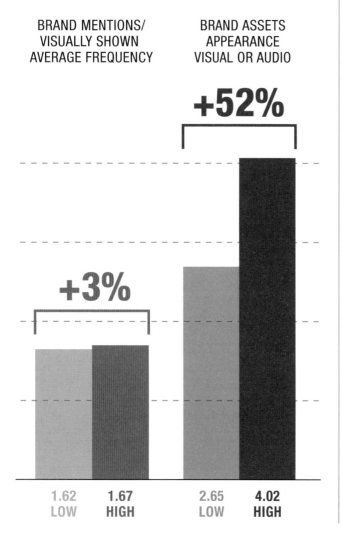

BRAND MENTIONS/
VISUALLY SHOWN
AVERAGE FREQUENCY

BRAND ASSETS
APPEARANCE
VISUAL OR AUDIO

+52%

+3%

| 1.62 | 1.67 | 2.65 | 4.02 |
| LOW | HIGH | LOW | HIGH |

Furthermore, when comparing the high and low performers by asset type, we observed an interesting trend, with assets the brand specifically invested in often more likely than an asset licensed or acquired to be related to stronger Brand Attention effects. An example is Brand Characters compared to Celebrities. Although celebrities are the second strongest visual brand asset in terms of being linked to a greater likelihood to be a high vs. low performing ad, advertising that uses Brand Characters is twice as likely as Celebrities to be high than low. The same difference is observed between sonic brand cues, that the brand itself invests in to create and represent the essence of their brand, compared to licensed music.

After identifying these trends, we then see value not only in the new and entertaining but also in the familiar. Delivering an original and entertaining, emotional experience of value to an audience does indeed have an advantage in encoding memories of the advertising, though there also appears to be a benefit in thinking carefully about using familiar Distinctive Brand Assets to ensure your brand is part of these memories.

In this respect, we see the value of combining the new with the familiar. We can also consider that Distinctive Brand Assets can inspire evolutions in the advertising experience, rather than only a means by which the brand can consistently and easily be linked

FIGURE 35: COMPARING HIGH AND LOW PERFORMERS BY ASSET TYPE

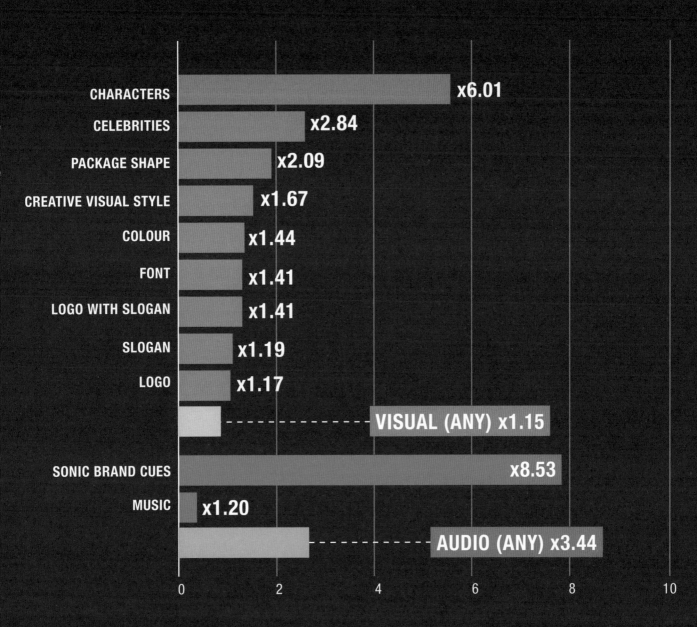

to encoded memories. An example we referenced earlier that used assets to great effect by inspiring evolutions in a campaign over time was Budweiser *Whassup?*, where the agencies used the *Whassup?* mnemonic to extend the experience from the friends in their apartments to people in other countries around the world, and even aliens on a spaceship.

KFC is another example of a brand using assets to inspire different creative directions. Their founder, Harland Sanders, after many false starts and struggles to establish his franchise business, recognised the value of distinctiveness, creating the character of "The Colonel", which he played to the outside world for the last 20 years of his life[56]. With a distinct bleached white moustache, white hair and white suit, people could easily recognise and retrieve memories of KFC when choosing a restaurant to visit or order take out from. The Colonel has also acted as a palette from which KFC as a brand has been able to access new audiences, with a recent example "The Hot Colonel", a younger, male model-like version of the Colonel that people can "date" in an app[57].

KFC has also reached and engaged with audiences in the UK by playing on the distinctiveness of their logo and linking this to the behaviour of their competitors. While logos have a weaker relationship with Brand Attention on average, their 2020 campaign makes it clear that KFC's competitors believe it is a valuable asset that can attract customers. With their creative agency, Mother, they brilliantly called out the appropriation of the logo to implicitly communicate the quality of their food and won a UK Bronze Effie in the process.

The logo has also served as a basis from which KFC could communicate to their customers during a challenging time in 2018 when they had supply chain issues in getting chickens to their restaurants. Most companies would have issued the standard apology letter, with words from the CEO to the effect of "*lessons learned*" and "*every step will be taken to get our services back to normal*". Not KFC. In fact, with their agency Mother, they turned a crisis into a moment of typically British self-deprecation and humour, with their inversion of the KFC logo to "FCK".

FIGURE 36: KFC "THE COLONEL"

Source: © KFC, The Colonel, 2019[XIV]

Across these examples, we see something in addition to the evidence of the value of distinctive brand assets in terms of end effects. Yes, they do seem to be closely related to more positive Brand Attention, by enabling the brand to more easily be present in encoded memories. But, moreover, they offer an opportunity to think creatively and differently in the advertising a brand produces, playing with established brand assets to take different approaches, thus further contributing to value for the brand, whether that is engaging with new audiences, or saying sorry in a way that will also entertain and bring humour at a challenging time.

FIGURE 37: KFC "GUYS WE'RE FLATTERED"

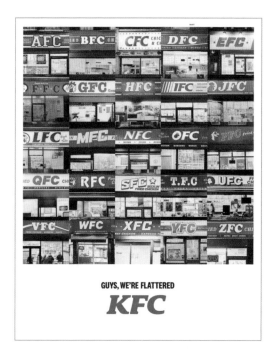

Source: © KFC, Guys we're flattered, 2019[XV]

FIGURE 38: KFC "FCK"

Source: © KFC, FCK, 2018[XVI]

XIV - www.wsj.com/articles/kfc-spices-up-the-colonel-with-dating-game-drawing-horror-and-delight-11569350129

XV - www.campaignlive.co.uk/article/kfc-takes-aim-pretenders-new-campaign/1579873

XVI - www.campaignlive.co.uk/article/kfc-fcking-clever-campaign/1498912

The long term value of not fitting in

As we have seen, although *Creative Experiences* matter in advertising effects, they are related most to Memory Encoding. They offer the price of admission to allow for the opportunity that the advertising has to influence choices in the short and long term. They are not strongly related to influencing these choices.

Instead, *Creative Ideas*, showing people "something new" and making them think "the brand is different" has the strongest link to Brand Relationship effects, the perception that the brand meets emotional and functional needs and is a good long term choice. This is followed by *Empathy and Fitting In*, emerging 15 points lower than *Creative Ideas* on the percentage increase in average change. So, while *Empathy and Fitting In* matters, *Creative Ideas* matter more to long term effects.

Why might this be the case and how does this relate back to what we know about people and how they process information and make decisions? As we know, people gravitate to the familiar, drawing on past experiences, often automatically, to reduce uncertainty and make the safest choice or behaviour. But as we learnt, people can sometimes be triggered by an external influence to switch to more deliberate thinking and change their behaviour. Any change is

often not instant as previous choices are ingrained and automatically referenced to reduce uncertainty, and at this point, we should return to the Misfits, the people who think differently.

FIGURE 39: ADVERTISING THAT INCLUDES CREATIVE IDEAS IS MOST LIKELY TO INFLUENCE LONG-TERM BRAND RELATIONSHIPS

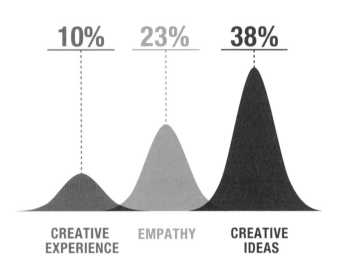

% INCREASE IN AVERAGE BRAND RELATIONSHIP CHANGE FOR ADS RATED HIGH VS LOW ON EACH DIMENSION

Source: Ipsos Global Creative Evaluation Database (n=1,734 cases)

From the Misfits we have profiled in this publication, it would not be farfetched to surmise that their different ways of thinking were not initially effective or successful. In Tony Hawk's case, he was bullied relentlessly; in Shigeru Miyamoto's, he was questioned vigorously in the corporate boardroom. Similarly in David Bowie's case, he re-applied outside inspiration from different sources over many years. But in the longer term, they were successful.

It is from these experiences and this mindset of thinking differently in a consistent way that we can consider advertising can deliver longer term effects. We've consistently referred to the fact that people are pre-wired to manage uncertainty, and that they often gravitate automatically to the familiar choices they have made. But people can also change their behaviour when triggered to switch to more deliberative processing, and the available evidence suggests that *Creative Ideas* are such a trigger in advertising effects in the longer term.

But what is meant by showing people "something new" or making them believe the "brand is different" from other options, and why does this matter to longer term behaviour and decision-making?

FIGURE 40: ICEBREAKER "THE UNCOMFORTABLE TRUTH OF WEARING PLASTIC"

Source: © Icebreaker, The Uncomfortable Truth of Wearing Plastic, 2021[XVII]

A campaign that epitomises the effects of showing people something new is Icebreaker "The Uncomfortable Truth of Wearing Plastic". In the ad, a car is seen driving to the top of a mountain range and what emerges is a man wrapped in clingfilm, carrying skis and hiking gear. He uncomfortably and clumsily walks up a hill to his ski resort looking rather unhappy and the audience is shown the following question on screen: "*Still wearing plastic?*". We then transition to a group of people skiing in the mountains wearing something different, merino wool clothing.

The ad is certainly entertaining and draws from the principles of *Creative Experiences*, though it also introduces a new proposition to the audience, that merino wool, a fabric not typically associated with being sufficient protection from the elements in snowy mountain ranges, is a more comfortable and equally sufficient option to plastic based clothing. In essence, the ad delivered value by telling the audience something new, something they did not know before, and Icebreaker can of course be the choice to meet this new option.

Another campaign that achieves tangible business value by leveraging Creative Ideas and showing people something new is KFC's "Michelin Impossible" in Australia. The campaign hinges on an idea that few people would consider the fast-food category to be a genuine high quality food option for prospective patrons.

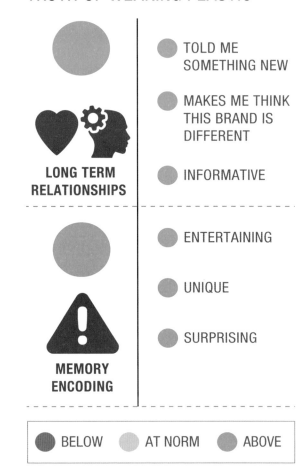

FIGURE 41: ICEBREAKER "THE UNCOMFORTABLE TRUTH OF WEARING PLASTIC"

LONG TERM RELATIONSHIPS

TOLD ME SOMETHING NEW

MAKES ME THINK THIS BRAND IS DIFFERENT

INFORMATIVE

MEMORY ENCODING

ENTERTAINING

UNIQUE

SURPRISING

BELOW   AT NORM   ABOVE

In the campaign, Sam, a KFC franchisee, sets out on an implausible mission to change perceptions of his food offering, from low quality "junk food" to what he and his patrons considered to be high quality. That mission was to get a coveted Michelin Star, and Sam makes the case that his KFC food meets the criteria of "Excellent cooking worth a special journey", with some patrons claiming to have travelled over 500KM to visit his restaurant in Alice Springs. The story continues with Sam speaking with a food critic and travelling to Paris to speak with Michelin representatives to further make his case for a Michelin Star.

While the campaign was undoubtedly entertaining and talkable, it is moreover driven by a near crazy Creative Idea to even attempt to apply for a Michelin Star and highlight that fast-food can, in fact, be high quality and worth travelling for. Despite being unsuccessful in gaining the Michelin Star, Sam and KFC's attempt led to tangible business results.

In their Effie award submission, KFC confirmed two thirds (65%) of fast-food diners agreed that "it improved my perceptions of the quality of KFC's food." Most importantly, sales increased by 7.6% against a category average of only 3.7%. As a result, the campaign won a Global Grand at the Effie Global Best of the Best Awards.

FIGURE 42: KFC "MICHELIN IMPOSSIBLE"

Source: © KFC, Michelin Impossible, 2021[XVIII]

FIGURE 43: RIMMEL "KIND AND FREE"

Source: © Rimmel, Kind and Free, 2021[XIX]

XIX - www.youtube.com/watch?v=pg8ldTSqpVl

Another example of a campaign that harnesses *Creative Ideas* and benefits with strong long term performance is "Kind and Free" for Rimmel. However, this campaign is more singular in its use of Creative Ideas. It is considered at above norm levels to be "unique" but is less reliant on being considered "entertaining". Yet it achieves a strong performance in influencing long term choices and behaviour.

In its execution, it uses a group of young, attractive models, which can be considered typical for the make-up category. But it does something different; it tells a different story about make-up and, in doing so, shows the audience something new, that they have not seen or considered before. That make-up can offer a "clean beauty", one that is kind to the skin of the people who wear it, and the planet, free of animal testing. In effect, the ad shows people there is an alternative to the make-up they currently buy, and they can look good without any adverse impact on animals and the planet.

In this campaign, we see an example of effective communication in action that talks about a more sustainable future. Less communication from a big corporation with a CEO talking about carbon reductions and the importance of a sustainable future, instead showing people an option they did not know about before that can help them play a part. This campaign and the example for Icebreaker then represent the power of *Creative Ideas*. That by showing people something new, something they were not aware of before and therefore adding value to them, the advertised brand can more likely than not benefit by being more likely to be chosen in the longer-term.

FIGURE 44: RIMMEL "KIND AND FREE"

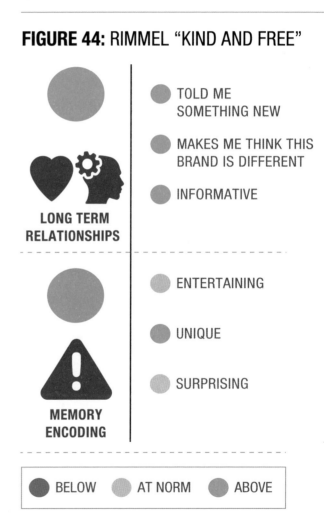

With Empathy, you can overcome Apathy

When considering the perceptions of the advertising experience that represent *Empathy and Fitting In*, we see little that links directly to our definition of creativity in advertising. The core of this experience is the perception that the advertising is directed at people like those in the target audience, that it depicts credible or believable events, and that it fits with how they feel about the brand. There really is very little that is "original" in this.

Let us though return to what we know about people. As we outlined, people are wired to reduce or remove uncertainty from their lives, and a frequently used mechanism to achieve this is to favour the familiar and gravitate to previous choices and behaviour.

Experiences where there is prior evidence that it was positive or useful increase the chance of a favourable outcome again, thus reducing uncertainty in the process.

It then stands to reason that if a new, entertaining experience that *does not fit* is the gateway to capture attention and encode new memories, that for those memories to influence choices in the short-term they need to also be grounded in the familiar, in something that *fits* their lives, their world, their challenges, their dreams. In essence, this is the role of good planning: identifying a core insight and reason to be for the brand, which in the execution of advertising can be communicated to connect with the target audience. A "people first" rather than a "product first" approach.

FIGURE 45: IKEA "NEW BABY"

Source: © Ikea, Home is where it all begins, 2021[xx]

When it does achieve this objective, we see that it has the power to influence short-term choices at higher levels than a *Creative Experience* and at similar levels to *Creative Ideas*.

An example of a campaign that takes such a "people first" approach is "New Baby" for IKEA in India. IKEA are well-known for their campaign strategy of communicating to people they can help make a house a home. This campaign reflects that strategy rather well. In the ad, a father and son are trying to play and communicate in silence, moving around furniture for a young baby, that we assume they do not want to

FIGURE 46: IKEA "NEW BABY"

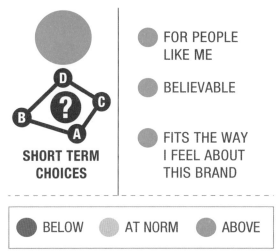

SHORT TERM CHOICES

FOR PEOPLE LIKE ME

BELIEVABLE

FITS THE WAY I FEEL ABOUT THIS BRAND

BELOW   AT NORM   ABOVE

FIGURE 47: EXPERIENCES THAT DELIVER CREATIVE IDEAS AND EMPATHY ARE MOST LIKELY TO INFLUENCE SHORT TERM CHOICES

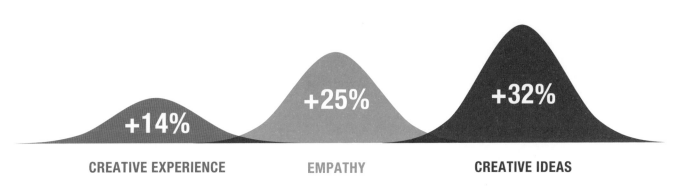

+14%   +25%   +32%

CREATIVE EXPERIENCE   EMPATHY   CREATIVE IDEAS

% INCREASE IN AVERAGE BRAND CHOICE EFFECT FOR ADS RATED HIGH VS LOW ON EACH DIMENSION

Source: Ipsos Global Creative Evaluation Database (n=1,734 cases)

wake up. We then transition to a moment where the baby is actually a doll and realise they are practising via play how to be quiet for when the baby arrives.

A heart-warming story that, in turn, has high potential to change short-term behaviour for the young family target, and one that is felt to be "for people like me", "believable", and "fits with the way I feel about this brand".

Another example of a "people first", empathic approach is Cass beer in South Korea. Beer advertising can often follow stereotypical tropes, focusing on refreshment and ingredients. While communicating a refreshing experience of the beer is not necessarily a *wrong* approach, what the "Real Summer Beer" ad for Cass demonstrates is it can be effective when you take a people first, rather than a product first approach.

FIGURE 48: CASS "REAL SUMMER BEER"

Source: © Cass, Real Summer Beer, 2021

This ad opens with what can be considered a quite typical scene in beer advertising: a group of young people on a beach enjoying themselves. But we then transition from this scene realising it was playing on a mobile phone near a car mechanic working in his garage. The mechanic is far from the idealistic image of the young people on the beach, sweaty, covered in oil and working hard underneath an elevated car. We move to scenes showing a student studying hard at her desk, a delivery driver carrying heavy boxes and a chef in a kitchen working over a hot stove. The ad then returns to each person with a friend offering them a can or bottle of Cass to give them a break, some refreshment and time with the people they care about. In this ad, we see less a story of good-looking people socialising together and more a reality of people working hard doing an everyday job.

Consequently, the ad performs strongly in terms of influencing short-term choices and is considered to be "for people like me", to be "believable" and "fits the way I feel about this brand".

Incidentally, this ad also performed strongly on Memory Encoding and Brand Linkage, demonstrating that an experience of *Empathy and Fitting In* does not necessarily need to be detached from a *Creative Experience*. That both types of experiences can work together to deliver incremental brand value.

A relevant example of a campaign that exemplifies the value of bringing together a creative experience with an empathic one is a Danish ad for the Volvo XC60. Car advertising can often suffer from being rather abstract, with the stereotypical campaign of the advertised model driving along an attractive looking mountain or landscape, but this campaign takes a different approach. It focuses on the people it needs to appeal to, in this case, young families with tired parents, a set of conditions that many are likely to relate to. In effect, it empathises with the experience of being a new parent and the challenges of adapting to life with a new born baby. The ad starts with the first scan at the hospital and arrival of the baby, then transitions to scenes depicting

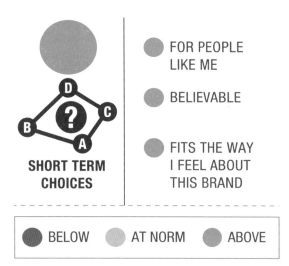

FIGURE 49: CASS "REAL SUMMER BEER"

FOR PEOPLE LIKE ME

BELIEVABLE

FITS THE WAY I FEEL ABOUT THIS BRAND

SHORT TERM CHOICES

BELOW   AT NORM   ABOVE

the late nights, the missteps the two parents make, the child proofing of their home, the night-time visits to the supermarket to get nappies and other baby paraphernalia. With many sleepless nights, we then turn to a scene when the mother falls asleep at the wheel driving home, veering into the next lane of traffic travelling in the opposite direction, when the car self corrects the steering and saves her from a likely fatal accident.

This is very much a people first approach to advertising, reflecting their world, their lives and the role the product plays in this, rather than blandly elucidating product features and delivering rational information. In effect, it leverages empathy to overcome apathy. As a result, this campaign performs strongly in terms of influencing short-term choices and behaviour.

FIGURE 50: VOLVO XC60 "THE PARENTS"

Source: © Volvo, XC60 The Parents, 2021XXI

FIGURE 51: VOLVO XC60 "THE PARENTS"

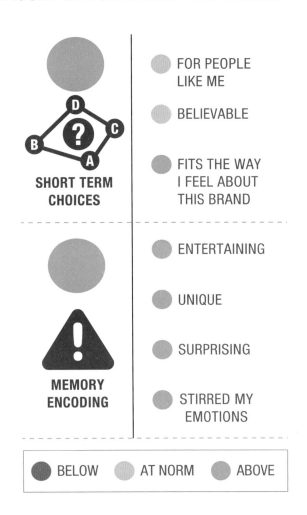

SHORT TERM CHOICES

- FOR PEOPLE LIKE ME
- BELIEVABLE
- FITS THE WAY I FEEL ABOUT THIS BRAND

MEMORY ENCODING

- ENTERTAINING
- UNIQUE
- SURPRISING
- STIRRED MY EMOTIONS

BELOW • AT NORM • ABOVE

The campaign also represents the nuanced, intricate effects of creativity in advertising. In addition to focusing on reflecting the real world of the target audience, in a relatable and familiar way, it also delivers a "unique" and "entertaining" experience. Which we know is linked to a strong ability to achieve Memory Encoding, the price of admission, and this campaign duly performs well on this key effect.

As a result of performing highly on Behaviour Change and Brand Attention, the Volvo XC60 campaign performs strongly on the Creative Effect Index (CEI), which is validated to end sales outcomes.

Another campaign in the Auto category that has empathy for people as opposed to a myopic focus on features is Subaru's "Rise to Safest" in the USA. Similar to Volvo, Subaru has recognised in a long-running campaign that they can benefit from showing the outcome of their safety features on the lives of their customers rather than talking about the features that can enable safety.

And they do this in an impactful way, with humanity and sincerity, by simply showing wrecked Subaru cars that have been in accidents and transitioning to scenes of families together that likely would not have been here if it were not for Subaru. In essence, a Subaru is an enabler of safety and quite literally, their lives.

The campaign represents a sadly uncommon approach in Auto advertising, where Subaru actively want to show their vehicles as wreckages instead of showcasing their beauty and technical features. Smashed, crushed and near unrecognisable, to make the point that cars can be replaced, people cannot. A far cry from most Auto advertising, which is often bereft of human interaction and empathy for the people car manufacturers want to appeal to.

Alongside Volvo, we see evidence that showing empathy for your audience has tangible business value. In its Effie submission, Subaru reported sales increases outperforming the category. With their commitment to this campaign idea and execution for over 10 years, this is importantly consistent over the long term. As a result, these effects were recognised with an Effie Gold award in 2020.

What this represents tangibly for the role of creativity in advertising is that it does not contribute in only one way, delivering an original and entertaining experience. Instead, it also delivers the strongest end business effects by delivering a new or different experience of value to the audience, in this case, doing something new in car advertising by representing the familiar and relatable life conditions of the types of people it wants to influence. This brings us to an example of two brands in the fast-food category that take quite different approaches to their advertising to get encoded in memory and influence choices.

FIGURE 52: SUBARU "RISE TO SAFETY"

Subaru.
More 2014 IIHS Top Safety Picks than any other brand.

2014 Top Safety Picks include the 2015 Subaru Forester and WRX.

Source: © Subaru, Rise to Safety, 2021

The most effective advertising puts the "Extra" into "Ordinary"

McDonald's and Burger King are the Goliath and David of the marketing world. Like David in the biblical parable, Burger King are well-known for taking a different approach to their marketing. Over time, they have developed a reputation for different and, at times, shocking marketing tactics to capture the attention of fast-food diners. The question is if a focus on leveraging difference, a core principle of *Creative Experiences* and *Creative Ideas*, leads to strong creative effects, and how does this compare to Goliath in the form of McDonald's?

One campaign for Burger King that has become synonymous with difference and divergence from the norm is the "Mouldy Whopper". This ad shows the Burger King hero product, the Whopper, decaying over time in a stop-motion sequence covering a period of 34 days. Over this time, the burger wilts and grows fur on the meat, before spreading to a rather unappetising plague of green mould, all with jewels of encrusted spores on the meat and salad in the bun. It is both beautiful to behold and disgusting at the same time.

And it certainly captures attention, achieving one of the strongest Memory Encoding performances we have observed in the United States, with people also agreeing the ad is "unique" and would be "talked about" well above norm. Moreover, the ad performs well on Brand Linkage, which is likely related to the constant presence on screen of a clear distinctive

FIGURE 53: BURGER KING "MOULDY WHOPPER"

Source: © Burger King Mouldy Whopper 2020[XXII]

FIGURE 54: BURGER KING "MOULDY WHOPPER"

MEMORY ENCODING   BRAND LINKAGE

 UNIQUE

WILL BE TALKED ABOUT

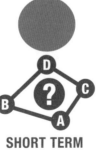

SHORT TERM CHOICES

BELOW   AT NORM   ABOVE

FIGURE 55: BURGER KING "MOULDY WHOPPER"

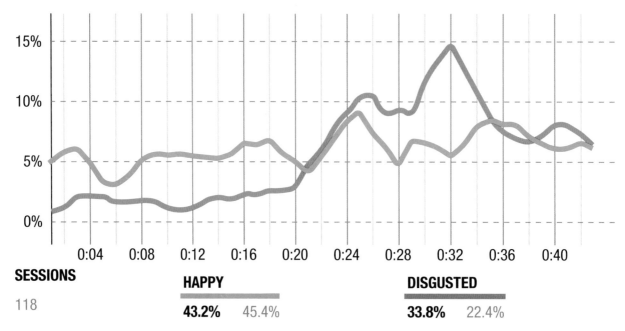

SESSIONS

118

HAPPY

43.2% 45.4%

DISGUSTED

33.8% 22.4%

Source: Ipsos, Breaking the Mould POV, 2020

asset for the brand in the Whopper. The uniqueness and talkability is, however, accompanied by an immediate emotional response that would not normally be welcome in a food ad, with the "disgust" response unusually higher than the positive emotion of "happy".

Normally, this strong Brand Attention performance is something to be happy about. If your ad is not encoded in the mind and linked to the brand, it is unlikely to have the potential to influence choices

and behaviour. The question is, does it capitalise on the attention it has won, especially with such an unusually high "disgust" response?

Based on the responses of regular people, this does not appear to be the case, with a below norm performance on short-term choice effects. Although the choice effect is low, this may not have been the core objective for Burger King. It could instead have been to capture attention and get people talking, which it certainly achieves. How though does this approach of shock and difference compare to the market leader in McDonald's and what can we learn from this about the role of difference in advertising related to other experiences, such as Empathy?

The first observation to make about McDonald's is that like many fast-food restaurant chains, Burger King included, they run a lot of product-focused and at times promotional campaigns. We will not focus on these types of campaigns which, despite their role in delivering end sales effects, are not a fair comparison point for the Mouldy Whopper campaign. When we look at campaigns that can be considered more focused on the brand, to get people to visit in general

rather than buy a specific item on the menu, we see little that is different, disruptive or surprising.

What we see from their brand campaigns is a more "people first" approach, one of empathy for the people it attempts to appeal to. One such example is "Laughter" in the UK. In this campaign, we see people laughing together, hugging each other and at times, crying together. First aired after the end of COVID-19 lockdowns, this campaign was geared to remind people of the emotional value of coming back together. In showing these moments of joy and laughter, McDonald's food and restaurants are nearly always present. But they are not the focus, they are the enabler.

FIGURE 56: MCDONALD'S "LAUGHTER"

Source: © McDonald's, Laughter, 2021[XXIII]

Another brand campaign in a post-COVID-19 world is "Steal My Fries" in Canada. In this ad, a diner is sitting at a McDonald's restaurant and breaks into song about how, given the time they have spent apart in lockdown, he would now be happy for his friend to steal his fries if it meant they could spend time together again. The musical song brings entertainment, while the theme in the "Laughter" ad of McDonald's bringing people together is also evident.

There is little disruptive or "different" in these campaigns, though equally, they cannot be considered the same as other fast-food advertising. They entertain, evoke an emotional response and create a point of difference for the brand to stand out from others by consistently taking an empathic "people first" approach where McDonald's is the enabler of human connection, over time.

Which approach though is more effective in increasing the likelihood the brand will be chosen over others? If we think more broadly than the archetype of Burger King's David to McDonald's Goliath, we see clear evidence that campaigns that deliver a Creative Experience or Creative Ideas that do not fit in *and* Empathy that fits in are more effective than creativity or empathy alone. By grouping the ads in our database in terms of high or low performance in delivering a creative or empathic experience, we see a clear benefit for leveraging both experiences *together*, with ads that do this achieving a +20% above average performance on short term sales, measured by the Creative Effect Index.

With these observations in the data, we see further evidence that advertising effects are not attributable to any singular experience or element. The evidence

FIGURE 57: MCDONALD'S "STEAL MY FRIES"

Source: © McDonald's, Laughter, 2021[XXIV]

FIGURE 58: CLASSIFYING BURGER KING AND MCDONALD'S CAMPAIGNS

	BURGER KING	MCDONALD'S	
CREATIVITY AND MISFITTING	**MOULDY WHOPPER**	**LAUGHTER**	**STEAL MY FRIES**
Creative Experiences			
Unique	X		X
Entertaining			X
Surprising	X		
People will talk about	X		
Stirred my Emotions	X	X	X
Creative Ideas			
Told me something new			
Brand is different	X	X	X
Informative			
Empathy and Fitting In			
For people like me		X	X
Believable		X	X
Fits with the way I feel about the brand		X	X

suggests you can have the best thought out and planned ad campaign with the target audience in mind, but you will more likely than not have mediocre business results without the magic of an original and entertaining experience. Likewise, you can craft an entertaining, unique, emotional ad, but if it is bereft of empathy and a "people first" approach, you will not be better than average. What we observe in this interaction is the value of early strategic planning and insights to underpin the type of experience you want to deliver.

And it is this interaction between creativity and empathy that brings us back to people. As we

observed, people are pre-wired to manage and reduce uncertainty in their lives and, unless there is an intervention that triggers deliberate thinking, they will often automatically gravitate to past experiences, even if it is not the most effective outcome they could have. Based on these findings, the most effective advertising finds a balance between the creativity of original and different experiences with something anchored in the reality of the target audience. Something relevant to them and their challenges, their dreams, their world.

This balance brings us back to the Misfits of the world, the people who think differently to achieve

FIGURE 59: ADS THAT LEVERAGE CREATIVITY AND EMPATHY PERFORM AT ABOVE AVERAGE LEVELS ON SHORT TERM SALES IMPACT

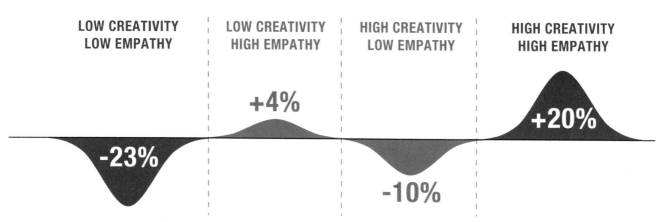

| LOW CREATIVITY LOW EMPATHY | LOW CREATIVITY HIGH EMPATHY | HIGH CREATIVITY LOW EMPATHY | HIGH CREATIVITY HIGH EMPATHY |

+4%

+20%

-23%

-10%

% DIFFERENCE VS. AVERAGE PERFORMANCE ON CREATIVE EFFECT INDEX

Source: Ipsos Global Creative Evaluation Database (n=1,734 cases)

more effective outcomes. The successful Misfits, Bowie, Miyamato, Hawk, the famously successful campaigns of Gold Blend *Couple* and Budweiser *Whassup?* all managed this balance perfectly. Whether it was riding the wave of smouldering romantic drama in popular entertainment or creating a new vernacular in culture alongside a relatable experience of talking on a call with friends.

This observed balance also connects with our proposed definition of creativity itself, *an original or different experience that is valued by the end audience*. Where difference, in the form of a creative, entertaining experience is the price of admission, and value, in terms of relatability and new ideas or thinking, have the potential to change choices and behaviour in the short and long term.

And true creativity in advertising lies in this process of connecting a creative experience and ideas with the more relatable and familiar. Perhaps this, more than delivering an entertaining, unique and talkable ad alone, is the real case for creativity. Advertising underpinned by people who think differently to combine a creative experience with a core, relatable insight and experience. Advertising crafted and commissioned by the Misfits.

Having made this case for creativity as a tangible business investment based on robust evidence, we will now outline how brands and agencies may benefit from applying these principles to pursue creative and effective advertising to grow brands in the final section.

FIGURE 60: ADS THAT LEVERAGE CREATIVITY AND EMPATHY PERFORM AT ABOVE AVERAGE LEVELS ON SHORT TERM SALES IMPACT

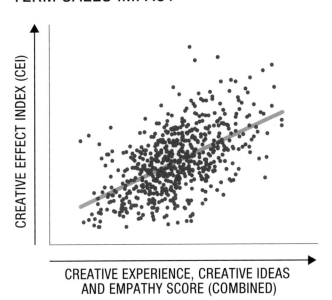

Source: Ipsos USA Creative Evaluation Database (n=647 cases)

SUMMARY

- Creativity matters in advertising. An original experience that entertains, evokes an emotional response and is expected to be talked about by other people is key for advertising to be encoded in memory. According to our hypothesis, this is because a positive, entertaining experience non-consciously opens the gateways in the brain to encode new information, as it will want to repeat this experience.

- No advertising experience identified is related to the effectiveness of linking the brand to encoded memories. Instead, the use of Distinctive Brand Assets can increase the likelihood that the brand is present in memories via visual and audio cues already linked to the brand, as well as inspiring new creative directions.

- Creative Ideas, where the audience is shown something new and the brand is considered different from other options, has the closest relationship with influencing choices in the longer term. Advertising has more potential to change choices and behaviour in the long term by showing the audience something new, making them aware of other types of service or product options, or issues in the world and solutions. This relates to a key principle of the Misfit mindset, identifying original or different solutions that can deliver end value.

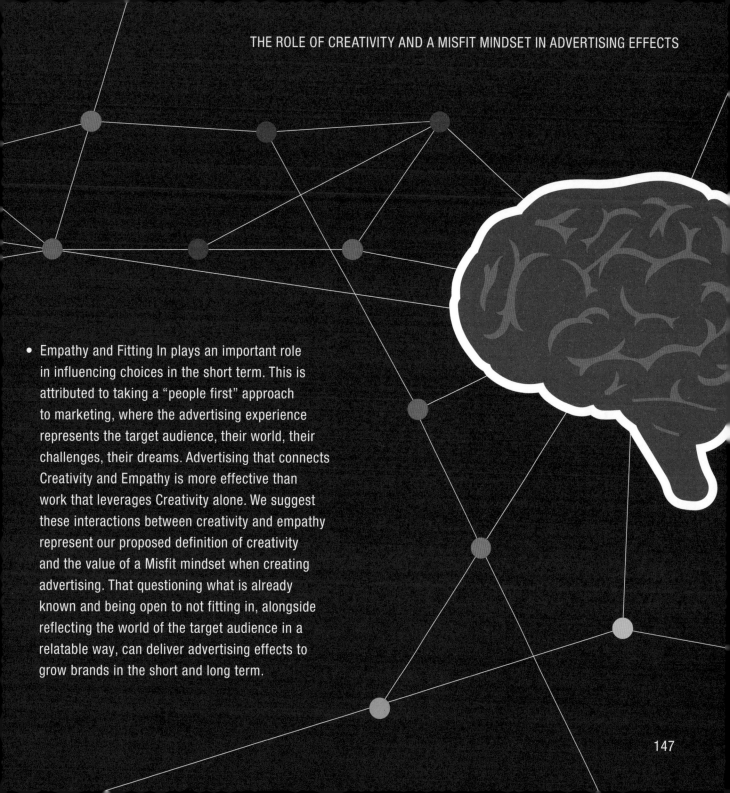

- Empathy and Fitting In plays an important role in influencing choices in the short term. This is attributed to taking a "people first" approach to marketing, where the advertising experience represents the target audience, their world, their challenges, their dreams. Advertising that connects Creativity and Empathy is more effective than work that leverages Creativity alone. We suggest these interactions between creativity and empathy represent our proposed definition of creativity and the value of a Misfit mindset when creating advertising. That questioning what is already known and being open to not fitting in, alongside reflecting the world of the target audience in a relatable way, can deliver advertising effects to grow brands in the short and long term.

HOW TO APPLY A MISFIT MINDSET TO GET TO EFFECTIVE ADVERTISING

At the start of this publication, we set out to define creativity in advertising and provide evidence for its value to end advertising effects. The proposed definition, *an original or different experience that is valued by the end audience,* helped us explore if such experiences naturally occur in advertising and if they have a relationship with end advertising effects.

With *Creative Experiences*, we observed the strongest relationship with Memory Encoding effects. That a unique, surprising, entertaining, emotional and talkable experience is linked to memorable advertising that provides an opportunity to later influence choices or behaviour. We referred to it as the price of admission.

With *Creative Ideas*, we saw the incremental value of new and different ideas in advertising to influence choices in the long term. And we hypothesised that these new ideas have this influence because they trigger more deliberate processing and, over time, have the potential to change behaviour towards a brand you may not normally choose.

But, like the human mind, the type of audience experiences related to effective advertising is complex. Yes, creativity has a valuable role to play, though the evidence suggests that it can contribute

to strong sales outcomes when it is connected to *Empathy and Fitting In*. The relatable, familiar reflection of peoples' lives, their world, their challenges, their dreams. And it is in the connection of creativity with the more relatable and familiar that we propose is the true definition and value of creativity in advertising.

This brings us back to the people who are responsible for the budgeting and commissioning of advertising. As we observed several times in this publication, marketers and financial officers are people. People are pre-wired to manage uncertainty and will often gravitate to the familiar and well known to make "safe" decisions. Data immediacy and abundance of the world of Martech managed campaigns and customer relationships is the safe haven many find themselves in today. A world where efficiency can at times be conflated with effectiveness and one where every advertiser has access to every system and platform, with little possibility in the future of a competitive advantage to grow their brands.

We believe this publication presents robust and generalizable evidence for the role of creativity and high-quality advertising to deliver end campaign effects. We consider that it builds on the good work of others in demonstrating that creativity matters in advertising. That a unique, entertaining experience anchored in relatable human insights relevant to the target audience will, more often than not, increase the likelihood of strong short-term effects, while creative ideas also have the potential to improve effects in the long term.

Our hope is if you are an agency planner, creative or marketer, you can take some of the data and argument in this publication to further **your case for creativity** and ensure advertising has the best chance to grow your business and brands. But how can you apply what has been learnt about the role creativity plays?

Given the topic of creativity, it would be ironic in the extreme, if we were to suggest "rules" and "formulas" for advertising success based on what we have observed in the evidence. Moreover, as researchers, we do not create advertising. We believe we have an important role to question, observe and highlight opportunities for creative agencies to pursue, but we cannot credibly outline exactly what should be done.

Instead, we should return to the Misfits for inspiration, those who do not fit in and, by doing so, often achieve more effective outcomes. We've seen that some key principles of a Misfit mindset have served famous Misfits well, whether this is experimenting to learn, blending the original and familiar, or looking to other parts of culture for inspiration to re-apply to their

work. However, what unifies these Misfits, and Misfits more generally, is a curiosity to question what is presented before them, to stress test the status quo and, in doing so, identify new solutions that can in time deliver more value.

This is what we submit: rather than turning to the observations of our research for answers and justification alone, you should use them as a foundation from which you can question your work at different points of the creative development process. To challenge yourself and the people you work with to get to more creative and more effective work.

We have outlined some possible questions you may want to ask. You may want to ask all of them, some of them or none of them, but we hope that even in reading them once within this publication, they can act as a reminder of what creativity really means in advertising. An ability to question what you are doing, to be open to not fitting in and to deliver creative and effective end advertising to grow your brands. In adopting this mindset, it is also our hope that this can help you to harness creativity in the advertising you produce more frequently and intensely. Because this will keep the house of the advertising experience intact by delivering brand growth and ensuring end audiences have positive, entertaining experiences that deliver them value.

LET'S *MISFIT* TOGETHER

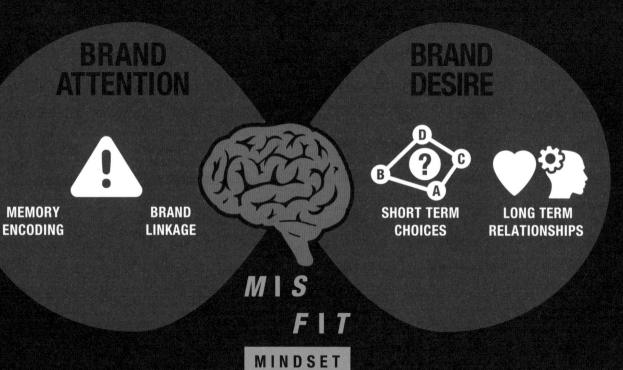

BRAND ATTENTION

MEMORY ENCODING

BRAND LINKAGE

BRAND DESIRE

SHORT TERM CHOICES

LONG TERM RELATIONSHIPS

MIS FIT

MINDSET

EXPERIMENT TO LEARN
BLEND THE ORIGINAL AND FAMILIAR
LOOK TO OTHER THINGS FOR INSPIRATION AND RE-APPLY IT

MEMORY ENCODING

- Have we seen this before?

- Are we trying to evoke an emotional response?

- Are we trying to entertain people and get them talking?

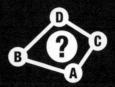

SHORT TERM CHOICES

- Is our experience relatable and "people first"? Does it reflect their world, their challenges, their dreams?

BRAND LINKAGE

- Do we know what our strongest Distinctive Brand Assets are?

- Are we using them to their full effect?

- Are they helping us create an original, entertaining experience?

LONG TERM RELATIONSHIPS

- Are we offering any new ideas and thinking?

- If we are, how do these link to people's lives and the role of our brand?

A WORD ON DATA FUELLED CREATIVITY

We opened this publication proposing that creativity in advertising, and the production of effective advertising more generally, is now allocated less time and resources than media placement. That advertisers have the risk of slowly advancing towards a singular, democratic destination where everyone uses the same tools to gain the same efficiencies, and no one gains an advantage over another in advertising effects to grow sales and market share.

While advertisers are investing more in Martech infrastructure and less in agency services to create advertising, the last few years have demonstrated the possibility that the media and creative world do not have to be siloed and compete for the same resources. That armed with the right strategy and vision, the Martech and data management infrastructure advertisers have been building can also be a fuel for creativity and contribute to effective advertising.

Burger King's "Whopper Detour" in the USA is a campaign that stands out as an example of using data as the fuel of creativity. This campaign turned the idea of a coupon redemption on its head, with a change to its mobile app, to offer a $0.01 Whopper coupon when people drove to a McDonald's restaurant, activated by geo-fenced GPS co-ordinates of their competitor's restaurants.

According to its Effie US Award submission, for which it won the 2020 Grand Effie winner in the Commerce & Shopper category, the app generated an ROI ratio of 37:1 revenue to costs[58]. Although we have considered "Mouldy Whopper" to miss elements of human empathy in its use of creativity, this campaign can be

FIGURE 61 BURGERKING "WHOPPER DETOUR"

Source: © Burger King, Whopper Detour, 2019[XXV]

considered to think about the needs of its audience more than just delivering a Creative Experience. Of course, being asked to drive to a competitor restaurant to redeem a coupon is an original and entertaining experience, but on top of that, it delivered value to people in the form of a near free Whopper.

Another campaign blazing the trail for data fuelled creativity is E.ON's "Let's Clear the Air" in the UK. In this multi-media channel campaign, E.ON set out to highlight the issue of air quality to communicate their commitment to sustainable energy, while also educating audiences about the invisible dangers of air pollution. They used a range of creative assets to communicate this message, including installing a 16ft set of lungs outside London City Hall. The transparent lungs were connected to sensors across London tracking air pollution levels and when they reached a danger threshold the lungs filled with smoke to visually represent the danger levels. They also used interactive digital out-of-home, where passers-by could stand in front of the unit to find out the level of air pollution in their immediate area.

Like Burger King "Whopper Detour", this campaign was both creative and effective. It delivered an original experience for its audience and value in reporting useful information about air pollution in their immediate area. E.ON also reported in its Effie Award submission, for which it was a finalist for the Internet & Telecom category, positive sales channel shifts[59].

While few in number today, these types of advertising campaigns represent a signal of a brighter future for creativity than the one we envisaged when considering the higher investments in Martech and data management infrastructure. That if the siloes are broken down by forward thinking marketers, data and media placement can indeed be an integral ingredient of creativity and the fuel of an original, entertaining experience that is valued by audiences, while also delivering sales and market share growth.

FIGURE 62 E.ON "LET'S CLEAR THE AIR"

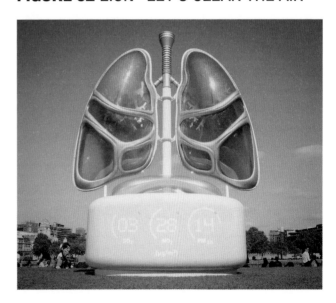

Source: © E.ON, Let's Clear the Air, 2019[XXVI]

We are also now seeing a recognition for the power of creativity in media, particularly from digital platforms. Previously in this publication, we painted digital platform owners as the purveyors of abundant and immediate efficiency data drawing attention and resources away from advertisers to produce good quality experiences for audiences. And while there is still a semblance of truth in this perspective, some digital platform owners are now actively supporting marketers and creative agencies to deliver a creative and entertaining experience to their audiences, possibly because they recognise it will lead to more effective outcomes for advertisers, and a more positive experience for their users.

One example is Meta's Creative Shop, a group of Creative Strategists available to advertisers to support the development of their ads across the facebook and Instagram platforms, and Meta's emerging AR ad formats[60]. Google's YouTube A B C D Playbook is another example, providing advertisers with guidelines to produce the most effective advertising while recognising the value of creativity to get there[61].

These campaigns and media platform initiatives signify the chance for a brighter future than the one we originally envisaged at the outset of this publication. That perhaps a Misfit mindset is not only the preserve of those who make advertising, and the data and technology people also have a claim to question the status quo, to help deliver creative and effective advertising.

We can only hope this is the case and, as time goes on, we will see more and more Misfits emerging across advertising production and media. Working together to deliver original, entertaining advertising that represents the people being targeted, as this will be good for audiences and good for brand growth.

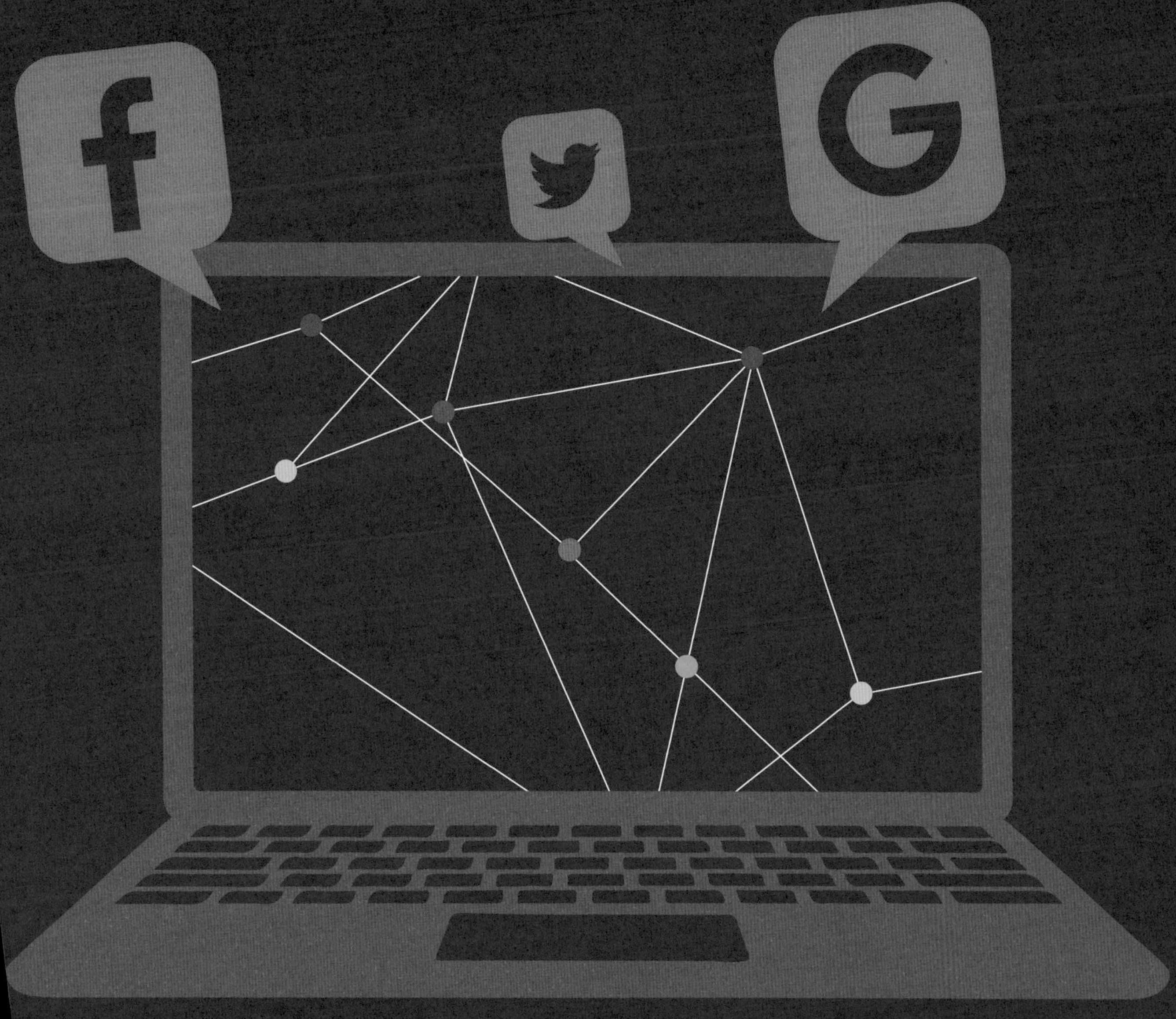
f
G

REFERENCES

1. www.pwc.com/gx/en/ceo-agenda/ceosurvey/2021/report.html

2. www.forbes.com/sites/bradadgate/2019/09/05/when-a-recession-comes-dont-stop-advertising/?sh=7cadab234608

3. A Critical Review and Synthesis of Research on Advertising in a Recession. Tellis and Tellis (2009). Journal of Advertising Research – April 2009

4. Procter and Gamble 2020 Financial Results (www.businesswire.com/news/home/20200730005458/en/PG-Announces-Fourth-Quarter-and-Fiscal-Year-2020-Results)

5. Annual CMO Survey – Feb 19 - cmosurvey.org/wp-content/uploads/2019/02/The_CMO_Survey-Highlights-and_Insights_Report-Feb-2019-1.pdf

6. Spencer Stuart CMO survey (www.spencerstuart.com/research-and-insight/chief-marketing-officer-average-tenure-drops-to-43-months)

7. Gartner CMO survey 2019-2020 - emtemp.gcom.cloud/ngw/globalassets/en/marketing/documents/annual-cmo-spend-survey-research.pdf

8. charleskochfoundation.org/stories/changing-your-perceptions-beau-lotto/

9. COREN, S. (1972). Subjective contour and apparent depth. Psychological Review, 79, 359-367.

10. www.ipsos.com/sites/default/files/ct/publication/documents/2020-09/dancing-with-duality-2020-ipsos.pdf

11. www.ipsos.com/sites/default/files/ct/publication/documents/2020-03/ddmm_-_gso_scientific_report_-_final_19-12-11.pdf

12. Predicting creative behavior: A reexamination of the divergence between traditional and teacher-defined concepts of creativity (Creativity Research Journal Volume 12, 1999 - Issue 1, V. L. Dawson, Thomas D'Andrea, Rosalinda Affinito & Erik L. Westby)

13. Factors Influencing Creativity in the Domain of Managerial Decision Making. Journal of Management, Vol 26, Issue 4, 2000 (Cameron M. Ford, Dennis A. Gioia)

14. Incentivizing Creativity: A Large-Scale Experiment with Tournaments and Gifts. ZEW - Centre for European Economic Research Discussion Paper No. 16-040 (Christiane Bradler, Leibniz Centre for European Economic Research, Susanne Neckermann, Erasmus University Rotterdam (EUR) - Erasmus School of Economics (ESE), Arne Jonas Warnke, ZEW – Leibniz Centre for European Economic Research)

15. mediatel.co.uk/news/2019/02/20/pricking-the-efficiency-bubble/

16. James Hurman (2016) The Case for Creativity: Three Decades Evidence of the Link Between Imaginative Marketing and Commercial Success

17. Albert, R. S.; Runco, M. A. (1999). "A History of Research on Creativity". In Sternberg, R. J. (ed.). Handbook of Creativity. Cambridge University Press. p. 5.

18. Csikszentmihalyi, Mihaly. Creativity: Flow and the Psychology of Discovery and Invention. Harper, 1997.

19. www.fastcompany.com/3047609/how-cannes-marketer-of-the-year-codifies-creativity

20. wklondon.com/2005/02/words_from_wied/

21. debalie.nl/programma/an-afternoon-with-oliviero-toscani/

22. medium.com/@Aaricia.wiesen/contextreseach-5c12de1d759c

23. Hegarty on Advertising: Turning Intelligence into Magic – 2011

24. Keep Listening to that Wee, Small Voice" speech by Leo Burnett. Chicago Copywriters Club. October 4, 1960

25. Why Does the Pedlar Sing? Paul Feldwick (2021)

26. Misfits Manifesto, Lidia Yuknavitch (2017)

27. www.grandviewresearch.com/industry-analysis/skateboard-market

28. Tony Hawk: What Marketers Can Learn | Talks at Google (www.youtube.com/watch?v=qrFESWVh1uY&t=1464s)

29. Originals: How Non-conformists Change the World. Adam Grant (2016)

30. www.slice.ca/the-20-wealthiest-skateboarders-in-the-world-2017-edition/

31. The History of The Legend of Zelda Series - From Pixels to Polygons www.youtube.com/watch?v=lwKJqPWLrUg

32. vgsales.fandom.com/wiki/The_Legend_of_Zelda

33. www.ign.com/articles/top-15-best-selling-video-game-consoles-of-all-time

34. thewaltdisneycompany.com/disney-to-acquire-lucasfilm-ltd/

35. Box office figures taken from the-numbers.com. Inflation adjusted to 2021 levels using smartasset.com/investing/inflation-calculator. Data detailed in Table 2 in the Appendix.

36. www.nytimes.com/2001/02/16/business/the-media-business-advertising-whassup-america-s-asking.html

37. fortune.com/2016/01/11/david-bowie-career-sales/#:~:text=140%20million%3A%20That's%20the%20estimated,sold%20worldwide%20throughout%20his%20career.

38. www.mic.com/articles/132265/here-s-how-david-bowie-influenced-queer-culture-and-helped-us-be-ok-with-who-we-are#.UEo5rxBpP

39. Inspirations (1997) – Michael Apted Documentary

40. David Bowie: Finding Fame – Francis Whately

41. www.bowiewonderworld.com/press/70/7409lkemp.htm

42. faroutmagazine.co.uk/david-bowie-aladdin-sane-cover-image-duffy/

43. www.theguardian.com/media/2003/jan/14/advertising.marketingandpr

44. ipa.co.uk/knowledge/case-studies/nescafe-gold-blend-love-over-gold

45. arstechnica.com/features/2005/12/total-share/4/

46. www.meaningful-brands.com/

47. Sharp & Romaniuk, 'Differentiation versus distinctiveness', in Sharp, B (ed.), How Brands Grow, 2010

48. Garcia-Garcia, M., Yordanova, J., Kolev, V., Dominguez-Borras, J., Escera, C. (2010). Tuning the brain for novelty detection under emotional threat: the role of increasing gamma-phase synchronization. NeuroImage 49(1), 1038-1044

49. Vuilleumier, P. (2015). Affective and motivational control of vision. Current opinion in neurology, 28(1), 29-35.

50. Rolls, E. T. (2017). Limbic structures, emotion, and memory.

51. Phelps, E. A. (2004). Human emotion and memory: Interactions of the amygdala and hippocampal complex. Current Opinion in Neurobiology, 14(2), 198–202. doi.org/10.1016/j.conb.2004.03.015

52. Davidson, R.J., Scherer, K.R. and Goldsmith, H.H. (2002) Handbook of Affective Sciences. New York: Oxford University Press.

53. Godard, Sheridan (2018) "Last Impressions Also Count". www.ipsos.com/sites/default/files/ct/publication/documents/2018-09/the_impressions_also_count.pdf

54. Kahneman, Daniel; Fredrickson, Barbara L.; Schreiber, Charles A.; Redelmeier, Donald A. (1993). "When More Pain Is Preferred to Less: Adding a Better End". Psychological Science. 4 (6): 401–405. doi:10.1111/j.1467-9280.1993.tb00589.x.

55. Sheridan (2020) "The Power of You". www.ipsos.com/sites/default/files/ct/publication/documents/2020-02/Ipsos_Views_Power_of_You.pdf

56. medium.com/lessons-from-history/the-tragic-life-and-struggles-of-colonel-sanders-2e1f685c34b5

57. www.wsj.com/articles/kfc-spices-up-the-colonel-with-dating-game-drawing-horror-and-delight-11569350129

58. www.effie.org/case_database/case/US_2020_E-5472-900

59. www.effie.org/case_database/case/UK_2020_E-452-879

60. en-gb.facebook.com/business/inspiration

61. www.thinkwithgoogle.com/_qs/documents/8472/ABCD_Complete_V7b_HR_1.pdf

APPENDIX

TABLE 1 THE LEGEND OF ZELDA GAME UNITS AND NINTENDO CONSOLES SOLD.

YEAR	CONSOLE	NAME	GAME PLAYING FEATURES	REPEAT OR EVOLUTION	UNITS SOLD (MILLIONS)[32]	CONSOLE UNITS SOLD (MILLIONS)[33]
1986	Famicom/NES	The Legend of Zelda	First open world top down gaming experience	NA	6.51	61.91
1987	Famicom/NES	Zelda II: The Adventure of Link	Reverts to a left to right side scrolling experience well known in the market	Repeat	4.38	61.91
1992	Super Famicom/ SNES	The Legend of Zelda: A Link to the Past	Moves back to top down free roam, and introduces time travel between parallel worlds	Evolution	4.61	49.1
1993-98	Gameboy/ Gameboy Color	The Legend of Zelda: Link's Awakening	Continues with top down free roam	Repeat	6.05	118.69
1998	N64	The Legend of Zelda: Ocarina of Time	New 3D game engine and "Z targeting" function to fight enemies	Evolution	7.6	32.93

YEAR	CONSOLE	NAME	GAME PLAYING FEATURES	REPEAT OR EVOLUTION	UNITS SOLD (MILLIONS)[32]	CONSOLE UNITS SOLD (MILLIONS)[33]
2000	N64	The Legend of Zelda: Majora's Mask	Same 3D engine. Released near end of N64 lifecycle with Gamecube release pending in 2001	Repeat	3.28	32.93
2004	Gamecube	The Legend of Zelda: The Wind Waker	New animation style and storytelling using a boat to travel between islands	Evolution	4.43	21.74
2006	Wii/Gamecube	The Legend of Zelda: Twilight Princess	New Wii motion controls	Evolution	8.85	123.37
2011	Wii	The Legend of Zelda: Skyward Sword	Same motion controls	Repeat	3.67	101.63
2017	Switch	The Legend of Zelda: Breath of the Wild	More expansive 3D free roaming world, more endurance challenges and expansive secrets	Evolution	23.2	84.59

Source: https://vgsales.fandom.com/wiki/The_Legend_of_Zelda32
https://www.ign.com/articles/top-15-best-selling-video-game-consoles-of-all-time33

TABLE 2 GLOBAL BOX OFFICE (USD) FOR FILMS WITH A SERIES OF THREE INSTALMENTS BETWEEN 1996 AND 2019, WITH AT LEAST ONE INSTALMENT APPEARING IN THE GLOBAL TOP 30 THE YEAR OF RELEASE. ADJUSTED FOR 2021 INFLATION.

FRANCHISE TITLE	1ST INSTALMENT	2ND INSTALMENT (% DIFFERENCE TO FIRST)	3RD INSTALMENT (% DIFFERENCE TO FIRST)
Toy Story	439,149,600	799,751,990 **(82%)**	1,339,046,977 **(67%)**
John Wick	99,431,093	191,438,514 **(93%)**	349,579,408 **(83%)**
Men In Black	427,176,678	672,006,399 **(57%)**	743,839,917 **(11%)**
Avengers	509,194,601	2,363,807,156 **(364%)**	3,046,478,946 **(29%)**
Hotel Translyvania	427,183,719	547,919,200 **(28%)**	575,627,730 **(5%)**
Fifty Shades	657,377,793	425,805,164 **(-35%)**	405,091,685 **(-5%)**
Ocean's	696,808,714	525,297,157 **(-25%)**	410,621,351 **(-22%)**
Despicable Me	681,608,051	1,139,679,290 **(67%)**	1,154,836,140 **(1%)**
Planet of the Apes	585,869,862	821,505,118 **(40%)**	547,643,256 **(-33%)**
Cars	626,911,133	680,780,514 **(9%)**	428,466,612 **(-37%)**
Thor	546,381,167	756,975,406 **(39%)**	953,038,473 **(26%)**

FRANCHISE TITLE	1ST INSTALMENT	2ND INSTALMENT (% DIFFERENCE TO FIRST)	3RD INSTALMENT (% DIFFERENCE TO FIRST)
Kung Fu Panda	802,947,336	809,481,814 **(1%)**	594,134,741 **(-27%)**
Taken	288,310,793	448,360,437 **(56%)**	377,409,887 **(-16%)**
Hunger Games	827,718,511	1,015,523,790 **(23%)**	873,192,358 **(-14%)**
Iron Man	744,000,500	783,036,330 **(5%)**	1,426,188,410 **(82%)**
The Hobbit	1,212,268,253	1,125,122,688 **(-7%)**	1,105,158,875 **(-2%)**
The Hangover	597,736,311	713,505,395 **(19%)**	424,988,085 **(-40%)**
James Bond (Craig)	822,341,446	749,356,793 **(-9%)**	1,321,404,727 **(76%)**
Batman (Nolan)	520,967,150	1,274,870,650 **(145%)**	1,288,601,214 **(1%)**
Madagascar	759,431,448	767,557,350 **(1%)**	890,330,159 **(16%)**
Twilight	517,535,586	905,030,014 **(75%)**	876,606,640 **(-3%)**

Source: the-numbers.com. Inflation adjusted to 2021 levels using smartasset.com/investing/inflation-calculator.